DECEPTIVE PATTERNS

EXPOSING THE TRICKS TECH COMPANIES USE TO
CONTROL YOU

HARRY BRIGNULL

CONTENTS

In memory of Mike Scaife, whose mentorship set me on this path.

ACKNOWLEDGMENTS

I am extremely thankful to the kind folk who reviewed early versions of the manuscript and helped me improve it.

Professor Yvonne Rogers introduced me to HCI and interaction design many years ago and taught me throughout my undergraduate degree, masters and PhD. She also helped me with this book. Thank you, Yvonne.

The legal response to deceptive patterns is rapidly evolving, especially in the European Union. While in no sense is this book a legal text, I would like to thank Dr Mark Leiser at Vrije Universiteit Amsterdam for helping me make some sense of the legal landscape for regulating deceptive design.

I'd like to thank Cennydd Bowles who spent hours helping me unpick and rewrite some of the more tricky arguments in the book. He also helped me with the first talk I ever wrote on this topic, more than a decade ago.

I'd also like to thank Finn Lützow-Holm who guided me towards lots of useful themes and research. It's become such a big area and Finn seems to be tapped into all of it.

Finally, I had a number of reviewers who asked to remain anonymous. You know who you are. Thank you.

Editor: Owen Gregory

Cover Art: Mia Brignull

ERRATA AND FEEDBACK

This is a first edition and no mistakes or omissions have been identified yet. If you wish to submit or review the known errata, please visit the webpage below. Similarly, if you work for an organisation that is mentioned in this book and you wish to provide a response, please use the same page. Thank you.

www.deceptive.design/book-errata

ISBN 978-1-7394544-0-1 Paperback edition

ISBN 978-1-7394544-2-5 Hardback edition

ISBN 978-1-7394544-1-8 Digital edition

Published by Testimonium Ltd

First edition: updated March 27th, 2024

PROLOGUE

Their faces give nothing away. It's a Thursday afternoon in March 2021, and the Communications and Technology subcommittee of the 117th Congress is holding a joint hearing online. Three of the world's most powerful people have been invited to give testimony in a session called 'Disinformation Nation: Social Media's Role in Promoting Extremism and Misinformation'.[1] Sundar Pichai, CEO of Google; Jack Dorsey, CEO of Twitter; and Mark Zuckerberg, Chairman and CEO of Facebook.

It's the moment I've been waiting for. The camera cuts to House Representative Lisa Blunt Rochester. She introduces the concept of dark patterns and defines them as 'intentionally deceptive user interfaces that trick people'. She asks Pichai, Dorsey and Zuckerberg:

'Would you oppose legislation that bans the use of intentionally manipulative design techniques that trick users into giving up their personal information?'

As the camera cuts to each of the CEOs, we see a stark difference. Lisa Blunt Rochester is sitting in a tiny wooden booth, connected with a grainy laptop webcam, but each one of the CEOs is evidently on a film set with professional lighting, cameras and microphones.

Picahi replies promisingly, 'We definitely are happy to have oversight on these areas.'

Dorsey replies with just three words, 'Open to it.'

Zuckerberg is more evasive. 'Congresswoman, I think the principle makes sense and the details matter.'

His reply seems to antagonise Blunt Rochester, who pushes him further: 'OK. Mr Zuckerberg, your company recently conducted this massive ad campaign on how far the internet has come in the last 25 years. Great ad. You ended with a statement: "We support updated internet regulations to address today's challenges." Unfortunately, the proposal that you direct your viewers to fails to address dark patterns, user manipulation, or deceptive design choices. Mr Zuckerberg, will you commit now to include deceptive design choices as part of your platform for better internet regulations?'

Zuckerberg hesitates for a moment: 'Congresswoman I'll… I'll think about it. My initial response is that I feel there are other areas that I think might be more urgently in need…'

Blunt Rochester cuts him off and gives a final speech, knowing her five minutes are almost up. 'If you say this is a desire of yours to address the issues that we face today – dark patterns goes back to 2010 – this whole issue of deceptive practices. And I hope that you will look into it! I will say […] our children […] our seniors, veterans, people of color, even our very democracy is at stake here. We must act and I assure you – we will assure you – we will act.'

A moving speech, but the CEOs are holding all their cards close to their chest. They know regulatory change is coming, but they don't want to give away any more than they have to.

———

Lisa Blunt Rochester was spot on in her statement. The concept of dark patterns harks back to early 2010. I know this, because I coined the term; though had I known it would become so popular, I would have taken a bit more care with the name. I remember sitting at my kitchen table in May 2010, ballpoint pen in hand. As I wrote about this topic for the first time, I was putting together a talk for a conference. *'I'm not sure there'll be enough here for a 20-minute presentation,'* I thought to myself – but the more I looked, the more I found. Deceptive tricks and techniques were in use all over the place and, at the time, nobody was talking about them.

A lot has changed since then.

PART ONE
DIVING INTO THE WORLD OF DECEPTION

In 2010, I defined a *dark pattern* as: 'a user interface that has been carefully crafted to trick users into doing things, such as buying insurance with their purchase or signing up for recurring bills'.

This definition is now a little out of date, and today I prefer to use the term *deceptive pattern*,[1] or to be pedantic, *deceptive or manipulative pattern* – but that's a bit of a mouthful, so in this book I'll use *deceptive pattern* as a shorthand to mean both.[2]

At the time, I was probably the only researcher looking closely at the area of manipulative and deceptive user interface design. Now, over thirteen years later, the area has blossomed into a multidisciplinary topic involving numerous human–computer interaction (HCI) researchers, legal scholars and many other people. Of course, I can't take credit for the work they've done; although I launched the initiative and defined a dozen or so of the initial terms, my role since then has mainly been that of an educator, campaigner and amplifier.[3] I've worked to spread awareness, to name and shame companies, and to encourage legislators, regulators and enforcers to take action.

To understand how businesses can employ design to manipulate users for profit, let's start with a physical example: travelling through an airport. When you travel through London Gatwick Airport, you're advised to 'arrive at least two hours before your flight to allow plenty of extra time to check-in and pass through security.'[4] But after you go through security at Gatwick, you're not allowed to go directly to the departure lounge. You're forced to do something that has nothing to do with your trip, and it consumes your attention, energy and time. You have no choice in the matter – even if you're running late.

The London Gatwick mandatory retail experience.

In the industry, this is known as a 'forced path' store layout.[5] It's really just a shop that's a long, winding corridor, packed into a rectangular footprint in the same way your gut is packed into your belly – travellers are forced in one end and come out the other. The curved path serves a useful function for the business – it forces retail displays into the centre of the traveller's vision, making it almost impossible for them to avoid looking at the stuff on sale as they navigate their way through the area.[6]

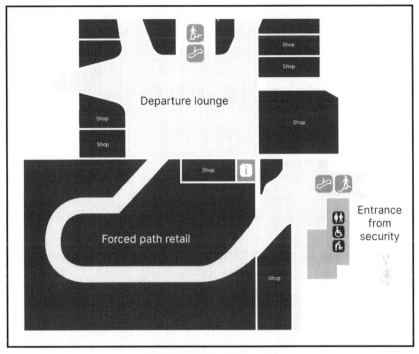

Floor plan of the London Gatwick South Terminal, featuring a mandatory forced path that doubles-back on itself.

Think for a moment about the airline tickets and legal terms. In those documents, there's nothing mentioned about requiring you to spend time in a retail area looking at perfumes, beauty products and alcohol before you're allowed into the departure lounge. And consider the airport's guidance – to arrive at least two hours before your flight. If time efficiency really was their top priority, they wouldn't impose the forced path retail store as a mandatory step between security and the departure lounge.

This is a good example of how businesses can use design to coerce and manipulate you. Arguably, it's also slightly deceptive in the way that the business is fully aware of the revenue-generating purpose of the forced path store, yet they don't mention it when they ask you to arrive two hours early, and they don't give you a shortcut to skip it.

In this example, the negative impact on travellers is minor and not particularly harmful; it's more of a nuisance than anything else. But when you consider the fact that over 40 million people travel through Gatwick every year, you can see why it's designed this way.[7] If this manipulative design can get just a few percent of travellers to make a purchase who would not otherwise have done, the airport can charge a huge premium on the lease for that retail space and enjoy a lucrative relationship with the retailer.

It's even easier to build manipulative and deceptive experiences online, because the designer has so much more within their control. When everything is virtual, anything can be tweaked to increase profitability. Here's a simple example of a deceptive pattern on a website. You've probably run into something like this yourself before when signing up to something:[8]

WIRED and Conde Nast would like to contact you with offers and opportunities. Please tick here if you would prefer to receive these messages:
by email ☐ by SMS ☐

If you do not want to hear from us about other relevant offers, please tick here:
by post ☐ by phone ☐

Our partners sometimes have special offers that we think you will find relevant, please tick here if you would prefer to receive these messages:
by email ☐ by SMS ☐

Please tick here if you would prefer not to hear from our partners:
by post ☐ by phone ☐

Excerpt from the Condé Nast Wired Magazine sign-up form (October 2010).

Did you see the trick? There's a switch in the wording between each line of checkboxes. If you tick the boxes in the first row, you're opting in to messages. In the second row, you tick them to opt out. Third row is opt in again, and fourth row is opt out. If you want to opt out but you're not paying attention, chances are you'll misunderstand at least one of the rows and end up getting spammed. This trick enabled Condé Nast to send out more marketing messages, which meant more 'eyeballs' – more people seeing the information – which in turn meant more sales and more profit. If you live in the EU or the UK, you probably haven't seen this type of deceptive pattern recently because it became illegal under the General Data Protection Regulation (GDPR)[9] a few years ago.[10] Hooray for progress!

Part of the inspiration for my work on deceptive patterns came from an interest in *design patterns*. A design pattern is a common and reusable solution for a problem when you're building user interfaces (UIs). For example, if I told you to close your eyes and imagine the sign-in box for a website, you'd probably see the same thing in your mind's eye as I do – a text field where you'd type your username, a password field below it, some kind of button that says 'sign in' and a link that says 'Forgotten password?'. That's a UI design pattern. Different industries have their own design patterns, and the idea originally comes from architecture in the built environment.[11]

Another well-known idea is the *antipattern*: a common mistake when trying to solve a problem. But as I sat there, back in 2010, doodling in the margins, I realised there was another type of design pattern that nobody was talking about. It wasn't about recommended practices or mistakes to avoid – it was about manipulative or deceptive practices that benefit the businesses that employed them and harmed the users who fell victim to them.

Although it's taken a long time, this area of work is finally achieving a breakthrough as new laws emerge. We now have the EU GDPR, Unfair Commercial Practices Directive (UCPD), Digital Markets Act (DMA),[12] Digital Services Act (DSA),[13] the proposed EU Data Act,[14] the California Privacy Rights Act (CPRA),[15] and the Colorado Privacy Act (CPA).[16]

The CPRA and CPA both use the same definition: 'dark pattern means a user interface designed or manipulated with the substantial effect of subverting or impairing user autonomy, decision making, or choice'.

Central to this definition is the concept of autonomy – for a user to be able to act according to their own goals, free from external influences, while understanding the nature of their choices. For example, if a user is tricked into sharing personal information because the legal agreement was completely hidden from them, then by definition there is no agreement: the user was denied their autonomy, since they were not free to become informed and make their own choices. However, the CPRA and CPA only cover privacy. The United States doesn't yet have any state or federal laws that directly address deceptive patterns beyond privacy. The EU is slightly ahead in this regard, with the much broader Digital Markets Act and Digital Services Act coming into force in 2023. The DSA uses the following definition (Recital 67):

> 'Dark patterns on online interfaces of online platforms are practices that materially distort or impair, either on purpose or in effect, the ability of recipients of the service to make autonomous and informed choices or decisions. Those practices can be used to persuade the recipients of the service to engage in unwanted behaviours or into undesired decisions which have negative consequences for them.'

As you can see, the DSA's definition is similar to the CPRA and CPA. It's about not interfering with users' autonomy, choice and decision-making.

There are a few different ways to think about deceptive patterns, and the legal perspective is just one of them. For example, if your background is UI design or engineering, you may be more interested in the mechanics of how they're put together. If you're coming from psychology or HCI then you may be more interested in how they prey on the human mind. If you're an ethicist then you may be interested in the broader philosophical implications. In the coming chapters, this book will touch on each of these perspectives.

My main point here is that deceptive patterns are not just a niche curiosity anymore. If you work in the tech industry you need to understand them, particularly since some types are already illegal, with even more activity coming from lawmakers, regulators and enforcers.[17]

Before we go much further, you'll need an understanding of how the design industry has evolved too.

CHAPTER 1
A PRIMER ON DESIGN INDUSTRY TERMINOLOGY

It's easy to think of design as how things look. Fonts, colours, textures, grids, mood boards – that sort of thing. This is *graphic design*: it's still important in its own way, but it's now just a small part of what the digital design industry has become.

Today, design is far less about how you decorate things, and far more about how you persuade and influence people into doing things. It's mainly about tracking, testing, psychology, behavioural economics, statistics and empirical scientific research. In other words, it's all about achieving business goals and making money.

You might not realise it, but when you use popular apps or websites, the details of everything you click on and scroll through usually gets recorded. Then it gets analysed, carefully. In big companies like Meta, Amazon, Netflix and Google, they have teams of people paid six-figure salaries, tasked to work out how to make more money out of you. Every day, your behaviour is tracked and you take part in quantitative research (e.g. 'A/B tests' or 'multivariate tests') to work out what will make you click, buy or agree to the legal terms. It's important to understand that the same research methodologies can be used to help or harm users. It depends on the intent of the business owner. It just so happens that deceptive patterns are easy to build and deliver measurable outcomes, so deception is commonplace unless a business owner takes a strong position on preventing it from happening.

Deceptive patterns aren't always the result of rigorous research and careful craftsmanship – sometimes they're just profitable accidents. Consider the example of a subscription offer that doesn't clearly explain the nature of the ongoing charges, just because the writer didn't take due care. This might result in a surge of revenue, which the business may then come to rely on, and they may not even understand why.

I'm going to use some industry terms in this book, so I'll define them here.

PRODUCT

This is the general term that's used to refer to an app or a website or any other piece of software that people use. The Amazon app is a product. So is the Facebook website. You get the general idea. Sometimes companies prefer to refer to their business as offering a 'service', particularly if it involves customers interacting with different people and numerous touchpoints over a period of time.

PRODUCT MANAGERS

In most modern organisations, a single individual is directly responsible for all of the decision-making for a given product or feature. This person is known as the product manager (PM). They're usually like a mini CEO, responsible for everything within the realm assigned to them, though the exact title and job description varies. If a deceptive pattern is created, then the PM of that product should know about it. They should know why it's been created, what purpose it serves, how many users interact with it and how it makes money. This is handy to know if you're ever involved in choosing who to subpoena in a class action lawsuit.

USERS

A user is the category of person for whom the product is intended, rather than 'all humans on the planet'. In the industry, we sometimes say *active users* for people who regularly use a product, and *target users* to include those for whom it is intended, but who might not be using it yet. The terms 'monthly active users' (MAU) and 'daily active users' (DAU) are also commonly used when measuring the success of a product, and deceptive patterns are often used to boost these numbers.

USER INTERFACE DESIGN

An interface is the point at which two things meet and interact. If you glue two pieces of wood together, the glue is the interface. In this case, instead of having two pieces of wood, you have a product and a user. The glue in the middle is the user interface (UI). With a screen-based device, we're mainly talking about text, images, boxes and buttons: these components make up the user interface. With a voice-oriented device, like an Amazon Echo, the user interface is the words or audio that comes out of its speaker, and the commands it recognises when you speak into its microphone.

USER EXPERIENCE DESIGN

A user experience (UX) is what you perceive or feel when you interact with a product's user interface over a period of time. If the interface is hard to use, then you'll have a negative experience.

However, not all user experiences have the same strategic goals. For example, when you pay for something online, you want the checkout to be pain-free and quick. Most form-filling experiences are like this – you don't want it to be fun, you want it to be done. In this context, usability and efficiency are paramount. Conversely, when you switch on a Nintendo or put on an Oculus headset, you want to savour every moment of the experience. In this context, emotions and entertainment matter.

Of course, there are many other kinds of human endeavour that need different design considerations. If you're designing an educational product, you need to understand how people learn. If you're designing the controls for an X-ray machine, safety is one of your biggest concerns. The list goes on and on. It's the job of a UX designer to think about these things. A UX designer takes a business's goals and marries them up with an understanding of user needs and user psychology. UX designers typically create sketches, diagrams and models – things that help with thinking and collaboration, forming a bridge between the people in the different roles in their team: product managers, researchers, technical subject matter experts and UI designers.

Unfortunately, the design industry has very few universally recognised certifications, or universally defined job titles, roles and responsibilities. Each company tends to use slightly different terminology and processes.

ALTERNATIVE TERMS FOR DECEPTIVE PATTERNS

Although the term *dark pattern* is still in use by some people, we should aim to phase it out and use more inclusive terminology that avoids negative associations. My preferred term is *deceptive pattern*, although if I am working with lawyers, I use the longer term *deceptive or manipulative pattern*, since not all of these patterns are deceptive. Various groups around the world use different terms to mean broadly the same thing:

- **harmful online choice architecture:** this term is used by the UK's Competitions and Markets Authority (CMA).[1]
- **asshole design:** a colloquial term, used on Reddit and other forums.[2]
- **dark nudge:** this term is sometimes used by behavioural economists, building on Richard Thaler and Cass Sunstein's term 'nudge'.[3]
- **sludge:** a term that specifically refers to obstructive design, which Cass Sunstein has written about extensively.[4]

It is unlikely we'll reach a universally agreed term any time soon, since this area of work now overlaps with legislation and regulation. For example, the word *deceptive* has a narrow technical definition in the United States at a federal level (due to the FTC Act), so the term *deceptive pattern* would be used very cautiously by US legal professionals (unlike in this book where I use it as a broad term).[5] Similarly, *dark pattern* has recently been defined in EU law, so it will continue to be used there despite its shortcomings. My view is that if you're not a lawyer or involved in legal systems, it's sensible to just be clear and descriptive about the design patterns you are talking about, and accept that there may be some movement in the terminology for this stuff as time passes.

CHAPTER 2
THE RISE OF DECEPTIVE PATTERNS

When I started working on deceptive patterns, I was a little naive. I thought they might be eradicated if we could name and shame the companies that use these practices. Or at the very least, perhaps we could encourage UI and UX designers to use a code of ethics that would reduce the number of deceptive patterns in existence.

This approach didn't work. In fact, things have become a lot worse since then. Deceptive patterns are everywhere now – there's even a tip line that takes reports from concerned users and relays them to policymakers and enforcers around the world.[1] The fact that we need a tip line at all means there's clearly more to do.

To be fair though, deceptive patterns didn't appear overnight. Deception is part of being human – in fact, it's so common in the animal kingdom that we can even think of deception as a feature of life itself.[2] The cover of this book features a Venus flytrap (*Dionaea muscipula*). This plant releases a scent that mimics the bouquet of fruits and flowers. Insects are attracted, and when they touch its sensory hairs inside the jaws, it snaps shut and traps the prey. This image is intended to be emblematic of unscrupulous tech companies who trick and trap their users using deceptive patterns.

Many historical stories and myths revolve around deception, such as 'taking the King's shilling'. In the 18th and 19th centuries, Britain spent a lot of time at war. But a career in the army or navy during wartime was not very attractive. With volunteers short on the ground, press gangs emerged to aggressively encourage recruitment, offering a shilling for every man who joined up. As the story goes, the act of receiving the coin was seen as a binding agreement, so unscrupulous recruiters would slip the coin into a sailor's pocket or tankard of beer. When it entered their possession, the deal was done, and the men would be forced into naval servitude. Myth or not, the analogy with deceptive patterns is a strong one. Whether it's clicking an ambiguously labelled button in a user interface or receiving a drink containing a hidden coin, it's obvious that there's a problem with the definition of consent if a person has no recourse after such a small, unintentional act.

It's useful to think about what makes commercial deception and manipulation different today versus the pre-internet era. There are some aspects of modern technology that have acted as an accelerant or a catalyst, intensifying and spreading these practices.

THE RISE OF METRICS-DRIVEN CULTURE

The idea of being driven by metrics dates back a long way: there's archeological evidence of accounting records from Mesopotamia, 7,000 years ago. Crude as it may have been then, human beings have got better at measuring things over time, and we're now fanatical about measuring things accurately.

What's changed is that the barrier to measuring things is now much, much lower. You don't need to be particularly clever or have a lot of capital to start measuring anything and everything you do in a business environment, and to start using data analysis to inform your business decisions.

In fact, metrics-driven management can be quite easy. You work out what metrics matter to your business, then you reward your teams for pursuing them using management techniques like performance-related pay, target metrics, bonuses and promotions. Of course, rewarding people for meeting a goal is almost the same as punishing them for not meeting it. In countries with less stringent labour standards, some companies use a management technique called 'stack ranking'. This involves rating employees according to their performance on various measures, arranging them in rank order and then getting rid of the lowest performers. If an employee's healthcare or immigration status is tied to their continued employment, this creates an enormous pressure on employees to do anything they can to hit their targets.

The web has also made it much easier to build and optimise deceptive patterns. With that in mind, I'd attribute the rise of deceptive patterns in software to the following general factors.

EASIER TRACKING

Before the internet, it wasn't easy to observe people without them being painfully aware of being watched. The traditional observation method was to send researchers to a store and have them stand there with a clipboard.[3]

But field researchers are costly and can only look at one thing at a time. Today, all you need to do is add a snippet of JavaScript[4] to your website to get in-depth tracking that observes every conceivable behaviour of every user of your product simultaneously, and have it recorded into a huge database in the cloud. Business owners have also noticed another advantage to online tracking. Despite it being more invasive than ever before, people don't feel anywhere near as worried about their privacy being invaded – because they don't feel human eyes on them. All that tracking happens behind the scenes, out of sight and out of mind.

Then you've got the data processing. Before the internet, it was paperwork. Thousands of pieces of paper. Getting all the clipboards together, transcribing notes and recording them in a ledger. Doing calculations by hand to work out how many people did what, when, and how that impacted the company's net income. Today, all of that calculation happens in the blink of an eye. Anyone can do it, using web-based software products like Google Analytics, Adobe Analytics, Mixpanel, Hotjar, or Amplitude.

These tools can give a wide manner of different insights: which ads or channels are driving traffic online, which pages are most effective at persuading users to take actions, the step in a series of pages at which users give up because they're confused or frustrated, and more. All of these insights are then looped back into the design process, where changes are made to the product to boost *conversion rates*: the proportion of people who complete an action compared to those who do not.

EASIER A/B TESTING

A/B testing[5] was first used commercially in the early 20th century, but in those days it was an awkward, painstaking process.[6] You could do it with newspaper ads: you'd run one version of your ad with a coupon, and another version with a different coupon. The version that won was the one that got the most coupons used. In those days, all the work was done by people; coupons delivered back to the agency were manually sorted and tallied by admin staff. It was a load of work and, of course, if your business wasn't all about advertising general consumer products to the masses, you were stuck.

The limitations of the physical world mean you can't apply the same kind of A/B testing to physical products and services as to digital without a great deal of cost and uncertainty. For example, if you have a shop on the high street, you can't change the store layout from one customer to the next. Perhaps if you were Cobb from the film *Inception*, you'd be able to click your fingers and rearrange your shop floor at a whim. In the digital world, *Inception*-like remodelling is trivially easy. You can make two versions of a page or feature and easily find out which performs better. For example, version A of a page might say '20 other people are looking at this item', while version B of the same page might say 'Only 2 items left in stock'. Your A/B testing software then deploys version A to a random sample of users and version B to another. After the test is complete, your A/B testing software will automatically calculate statistics for you, telling you if either of the designs performed significantly better than the other on the measured conversion rate (purchases completed, for instance). You don't even need to understand the statistics, as the results are usually dumbed down into simple sentences for you. No magic, cement, bricks or PhD needed. In fact, creating an A/B test today is as simple as signing up to a product like VWO or Optimizely free of charge and filling in a few forms.

A/B testing doesn't judge whether a particular design is actually better or worse for the user – it just provides statistics as to whether design A or B performed better on your chosen metric. This means A/B testing opens a door towards deceptive patterns, because when a business tests a deceptive pattern against a more neutral pattern, typically it's found to perform better on the chosen metric. Why? Because tricking or trapping users can be more effective than persuading them; and also because persuasion is frequently *combined with* deception, which means the overall page has two shots at capturing the user. It can start out by trying to persuade the user to complete the desired action. Then, if the user isn't successfully persuaded, the deceptive pattern has a chance to get them to complete the desired action through nefarious means. Imagine some persuasive content followed by a preselected checkbox, for example. Some users will be persuaded by the content and will be happy with the default. Others won't be persuaded and also won't notice the preselected checkbox, so they'll end up being tricked into opting into something they didn't want.

When a deceptive pattern wins an A/B test, it's often a direct source of revenue, with statistics to prove its effectiveness. In a metrics-driven environment, it can be very hard for employees to push back against this and encourage a more user-friendly – but less profitable – approach.

COPYCAT DESIGN

It was Oscar Wilde who said, 'Imitation is the sincerest form of flattery that mediocrity can pay to greatness'. Some tech companies have been very successful in driving up conversion rates by using deceptive patterns. In response, others have copied them. This isn't at all surprising. If you saw a competitor successfully making money for years without any legal or regulatory consequences, then why wouldn't you copy them?

CHAPTER 3
FROM HOMO ECONOMICUS TO HOMO MANIPULABLE

To understand deceptive patterns, we need to understand some concepts from the field of economics. For a long time, economists believed humans were perfect information-processing machines – able to consume, understand and reason with all the information provided to them at all times. They called this idea 'homo economicus'. If you think about the number of mistakes we all make in our daily lives, you'll know this is a really daft idea. Still, it's understandable. Economists needed to start somewhere, and they also needed to start with a relatively simple model of how humans behave, otherwise the maths gets really complicated.

It's only relatively recently – in the late 20th century – that economists have updated their views. It was considered groundbreaking when Herbert Simon introduced the idea of 'bounded rationality'.[1] He posited that 'both the knowledge and the computational power of the decision maker are severely limited' and 'we must distinguish between the real world and the actor's perception of it and reasoning about it'. In other words, we can only remember a certain amount of stuff before we start forgetting; we can only do a certain level of mental arithmetic before we get it wrong; and we can only read so much complex text before we become fatigued and start to misunderstand things.

To be even more reductionist, bounded rationality means we muddle through life doing our best with limited faculties. As someone who once fell down the stairs at night because I had forgotten that I'd moved house, I can attest to that.

More recently, behavioural economics has greatly extended the idea of bounded rationality. Richard Thaler is considered one of the founders of behavioural economics, and he won the Nobel prize in 2017 for 'incorporating psychologically realistic assumptions into analyses of economic decision-making'.[2] It turns out that understanding the ways in which people can do dumb things is really useful for economic modelling. Particularly when it comes to understanding the causes of the common mistakes we all make.[3]

'Real people have trouble with long division if they don't have a calculator, sometimes forget their spouse's birthday [...]. They are not homo economicus; they are homo sapiens.'

—THALER AND SUNSTEIN (2008)

Physically, our bodies have lots of common flaws. For example, the trachea and oesophagus are very close to each other. Most of us are familiar with the dangers of accidental choking. Knowing that flaw and sharing the knowledge has helped humanity a great deal. The same applies to human reasoning and decision-making. If we can understand ourselves better, the more likely it is that we'll be in a position to overcome our weaknesses.

Most psychology researchers and theorists are motivated by this honourable goal: improving the human condition. There's even a branch of applied psychology – human factors and ergonomics – which aims to 'reduce human error, increase productivity, and enhance safety and comfort'.[4] In a nutshell, the aim is to understand how the human mind works, and then use those insights to help people make better decisions.

Unfortunately, not everyone is motivated by kindness. Some see human weakness as a commercial opportunity. Instead of thinking of humans as homo economicus, it is perhaps more useful to think of us as 'homo manipulable': imperfect and vulnerable to control by others in ways we may not even notice.[5]

To recap, this chapter has explored the rise of deceptive patterns in the digital world and the reasons behind their ubiquity. Several key factors are identified as contributing to the proliferation of deceptive patterns, including the emergence of a metrics-driven culture, the ease of tracking and data processing, the widespread use of A/B testing, and the prevalence of copycat design in the tech industry. Over the past few decades, well-intentioned academic research has revealed weaknesses in human reasoning and decision-making. Today, these insights are used to manipulate users for profit, which is a far cry from the original intent of the research.

PART TWO
EXPLOITATIVE STRATEGIES

There are lots of different ways you can consider the underlying psychology and principles behind deceptive patterns. A good starting point is to think of them as the result of an exploitative business strategy. In other words, instead of a business thinking of its users as partners who should be cooperated with to reach mutual success ('Their success is our success'), the business thinks of its users as a commodity to be exploited ('Their weakness is our opportunity'). Another aspect of the exploitative mindset is the business's attitude towards law: rather than seeing it as a system to be respected, the law might be seen as a game to be played, where loopholes and grey areas can be identified and exploited for profit.

	Exploitative "Your weakness is our opportunity"	Cooperative "Your success is our success"
Attitude to users	User as commodity	User as human
	Vulnerabilities exploited for profit	Vulnerabilities supported with care
Attitude to the law	Law as game to be played	Law as system to be respected
	Loopholes as growth opportunity	Loopholes as pitfalls to avoid
Result	**Deceptive patterns**	**User-centred patterns**

A comparison between exploitative and cooperative design strategies.

If we look at it in a simplistic way, exploitative strategies are often going to be more effective than cooperative strategies because they sidestep the need to let users make an informed choice. It's a bit like wondering whether a fishing net is going to be more effective than just *asking* fish to jump into your boat. The fishing net is a trap, similar to a deceptive pattern. If you impede a user's ability to make an informed choice, or if you hinder their decision-making by hiding facts or by giving misleading information, then you effectively capture or lock in the user against their will (though they may not realise it at the time owing to a lack of clearly stated information).

Generally, businesses do not admit to themselves that they are using exploitative strategies. If a business focuses on growth and measured outcomes, it can slip into an exploitative mindset without realising it. Euphemisms are also very common in businesses (for example, a subscription that automatically renews without an email reminder might be glossed as 'We are helping users enjoy an uninterrupted service'), and the true consequences of a design decision may be far away from the people who implement it. In large tech companies, customer service teams are often outsourced overseas, far from head-quarters where the decision-making happens. When users are presented as charts and data dashboards in executive meetings, their humanity is stripped away, and it's easy to slip into thinking of them as just numbers, a commodity to be processed and from which value is extracted.

The best way to explain deceptive patterns is to start by looking at the exploitative design strategies – so you come to understand the theory, principles and goals – and then look at the result of the strategies, so you can then have a good basis for understanding the specific types and examples of deceptive patterns in the wild.

Professor Colin M. Gray and their team at Purdue University's UXP2 Lab were among the first researchers to look closely at the exploitative design strategies that lead to deceptive patterns.[1] Expanding on their work, I present eight types of exploitative design strategy in this chapter. These are summarised below.

- **Exploiting perceptual vulnerabilities:** Before a human can reason about information, they have to perceive it first. Since human perception is not perfect, the shortcomings can be exploited to hide information, e.g. low contrast, small text.
- **Exploiting vulnerabilities in comprehension:** Humans have limits to literacy, numeracy, critical thinking and memory. An exploitative designer can make something more complicated than it needs to be, e.g. the use of verbose terms and conditions.
- **Exploiting vulnerabilities in decision-making:** Cognitive biases are systematic errors in reasoning that all humans tend to make. They can be exploited to interfere with decision-making, e.g. a preselected checkbox can take advantage of the default effect.
- **Exploiting expectations:** Helpful design involves employing standards to make a product predictable for users. These standards can be subverted to trick users, e.g. making an 'X' button mean 'yes' instead of 'no'.
- **Resource depletion and pressure:** Humans have a limited supply of attention, energy and time. Once these resources become depleted, users may give up; they may feel pressure; and they may become fatigued and vulnerable to other tricks, e.g. cookie consent dialogs often require extreme effort to opt out, wearing users down until they give in.
- **Forcing and blocking:** 'Forcing' involves putting a mandatory step in front of the action the user wants to complete, which they cannot decline, e.g. mandatory registration in order to complete a purchase. 'Blocking' involves the outright removal of a feature, e.g. preventing the user from exporting their own data.
- **Exploiting emotional vulnerabilities:** Humans do not like to experience uncomfortable emotions like guilt, shame, fear or regret, and will often take measures to avoid them, e.g. to decline an offer for a fitness course, the user must click 'No thanks, I want to be unhealthy.'

- **Exploiting addiction:** Humans are prone to addiction, where a habit develops harmful outcomes and becomes difficult to give up. This involves a cycle of behaviour that can be intensified through design techniques like infinite scroll or autoplay.

CHAPTER 4
EXPLOITING PERCEPTUAL VULNERABILITIES

Before a human can reason about information, they first have to perceive it. With so much of our lives being online and on-screen, it is useful to consider how visual perception works.

Although it's tempting to consider healthy human eyes as perfect high-definition cameras, they are actually very different.[1] In fact, much of what we visually perceive is fabricated by the perceptual systems in the brain, and our eyes provide highly incomplete information. For example, the human eye has a physical blind spot at the back, where the optic nerve connects the eyeball to the brain. People with normal vision do not see any blind spot, despite it being present at all times. It's filled in by our visual cortex.[2] In simple terms, the human visual perception system guesses at what should be present and fabricates it. Or in other words, our brains are making it up as we go along.

In the same way, the middle of the retina contains sensors called cones that enable us to see in colour. Around the periphery of the retina we mainly have a different type of receptor called rods, which provide non-colour vision, and work better in low light. Yet we do not perceive any variation in the colour of what we see from the centre to the periphery of our field of vision. The human visual cortex does an enormous amount of 'guesswork' to fill in the gaps, making an inconsistent data source seem utterly full colour and high definition.

What's more, when a person with normal vision looks at something, they usually perceive a steady, fixed scene. However, the human eyeball typically moves around a great deal. When we read something or scan our surroundings, our eyes rapidly flick from here to there and back again, taking in all kinds of pieces of information in addition to what we're focused on. The fast movements are called *saccades*, and they last somewhere between 20 and 200 milliseconds. They're interspersed by *fixations*, when the eye stops, briefly, for 50 to 600 milliseconds. Yet we don't get motion sickness from it – we don't notice it at all.

To summarise, what you 'see' as a human is not reality, but an internal representation of reality involving imperfect sensors (our eyes) and an enormous amount of internal processing that uses amazing guesswork to fill in the gaps. This means that the entire visual system is exploitable, making it easy to hide things. In other words, camouflage.

A famous example of camouflage in nature is the lime hawk-moth (*Mimas tiliae*),[3] which has evolved to blend into its environment using colours and visual contrast to mimic its background and to create false edges that disrupt its shape, thereby avoiding visual detection by predators when positioned on a lime tree or similar vegetation.[4]

Visual camouflage used by a lime hawk-moth.

With apps and websites, exploitative designers frequently use similar techniques, by manipulating text colour contrast and size.

The interesting thing about colour contrast is that it is straightforward to calculate.[5] You capture the hex codes for the text foreground and background colours, then enter the values into a calculator tool.[6] There is an internationally recognised standard for minimum colour contrast: the W3C's Web Content Accessibility Guidelines (WCAG 2.1). It has three levels. The middle level, 'AA', is widely recognised as the baseline to aim for.[7] This means you can use a colour contrast calculator tool to instantly work out if a piece of text on a page meets the baseline recommended level for colour contrast.

One trick to watch out for is differences in text contrast on a page. If most of the text on a page is relatively high-contrast and one bit of text is relatively low-contrast, this could make readers less likely to notice or pay attention to the lower-contrast text, even if it is AA-level compliant. Readers often interpret colour contrast as a signal of what they should read versus what they can safely ignore (i.e. 'this pale grey text can't be very important – if it was, they'd have made it more prominent').

One of the first cases I worked on as an expert witness was Arena vs Intuit Inc.[8] In 2019, a law firm called Stueve Siegel Hanson approached me and asked me to review the account creation and sign-in process relating to Intuit's TurboTax products. A screenshot of the sign-up page is shown below. See if you can spot any issues, based on what we've talked about in this section.

One Account.
Everything Intuit.

One account for everything Intuit, including
TurboTax. Learn more

Email address

[   ]

User ID

[   ]

Phone (recommended)

[   ]

Standard call, messaging or data rates may apply.

Password

[🔓]

[🔒 Create Account]

By clicking Create Account, you agree to the
TurboTax Terms of Service, Turbo Terms of Use
and have read and acknowledge our Privacy Statement.

Screenshot of the TurboTax sign-up page in November 2019.

You might not realise it by looking at the screenshot in the figure above, but if you clicked the 'Create Account' button, you would be agreeing to binding arbitration. In other words, you would be unable to take Intuit to court. To find the information about arbitration, you are expected to notice and read the text below the big button ('By clicking Create Account…').

In my analysis I found that the colour contrast of that text was lower than most of the other text on the page, and the font size was smaller too. I can't write too much since a good deal of my report is confidential, but the key point here is that the judge agreed with this analysis. To quote:

> '…both the notice and the hyperlinks therein are in the lightest font on the entire sign-in screen […] The Court finds that a reasonable consumer would be less likely to notice text in a significantly fainter font than other text on the same page.'
>
> —CHARLES R BREYER, UNITED STATES DISTRICT JUDGE, 12 MARCH 2020

During the case, Intuit were required to disclose their analytics data, which showed that less than 0.55% of users actually clicked on the relevant hyperlink during a four-month period in 2019.[9] This is compelling evidence, and also a reminder that internal company data or documents can end up being revealed in a lawsuit, and it's sometimes the job of an expert witness to suggest what to ask for.

To summarise, small low-contrast text is an effective way to hide content on a page, and to prevent users from subsequently comprehending it and making an informed decision. Like many other exploitative strategies, manipulation of perception may be illegal in some jurisdictions depending on the way you use it.[10]

Another more brazen approach to exploiting perception is to remove something entirely from the user's perceptual field. If you don't want people to comprehend something, you just don't show it on the page, and you put it behind links or buttons that allude to something else. This is a very common practice in cookie consent dialogs – where the first thing the user sees gives no clue that there may be a button somewhere that allows them to reject all forms of tracking. In 2020, Nouwens et al. carried out a research study to measure the impact of this.[11] Forty participants took part in an online field experiment. Results showed that removing the 'Reject all' button from the first page of a consent pop-up increased consent by up to 23 percentage points.

In another study, the UK government's Behavioural Insights Team (BIT, aka 'the nudge unit') worked with an Australian government department to improve payment rates for fines, debts and taxes.[12] They sent two different letters to 48,445 people. In one letter, they featured a large red 'pay now' stamp on the letter, shown below. The other letter didn't have this stamp.[13]

Example of a letter with a 'pay now' stamp from a similar study by BIT.

They found that the letter with the 'pay now' stamp delivered a 3.1 percentage point increase (14.7% payment rate without the 'pay now' stamp; 17.8% payment rate with it).[14] We can look at that figure the other way around: the letter *without* the 'pay now' stamp delivered far *fewer* payments. So the simple act of removing a call to action is very effective. If someone doesn't perceive something – such as the need to act, or a reason to do something – they are less likely to think about it. If they don't think about it, it won't influence their decision-making.

There are other ways to manipulate perception that I should mention before we move on to the next type of strategy. Most commonly, exploitative designers employ clutter and noise – subverting common graphic design principles like white space, repetition, alignment and proximity. (If you're not familiar with these principles, any introductory textbook can provide you with a beginners guide.[15]) This serves to create a sort of smokescreen, making elements of the page harder to see, read and scan: playing into the exploitation of expectations strategy and the exploitation of vulnerabilities in comprehension strategy.

CHAPTER 5
EXPLOITING VULNERABILITIES IN COMPREHENSION

LITERACY, NUMERACY AND PROBLEM SOLVING

In 2013, a huge worldwide study called the Program for the International Assessment of Adult Competencies (PIAAC) was published, involving over 165,000 working-age adults in 23 different countries.[1] It looked at literacy, numeracy and problem-solving proficiencies across the world. The following summary is just for the United States, though the picture is fairly similar in many countries. According to the 2013 PIAAC findings:[2]

- 30% of adults in the US are likely to have difficulty sorting through emails and organising them in folders provided for them.
- 20% of adults in the US are unlikely to find the name of a congressperson with a summary information sheet that lists the district, name, year and place of birth.
- 30% of adults in the US are unlikely to be able to calculate the total cost of daily car rental when provided with miles driven that day, cost per day and cost per mile.

- 16% of adults in the US are digitally illiterate, and cannot use a computer to find a recipe, make a retail purchase or file taxes online.

As you can see, low literacy and numeracy is very common. With an exploitative mindset, this presents an exploitable vulnerability. If a business wants to hide unfair or unappealing aspects of a transaction, it can do so through the use of complex language or complex numerical content. With this in mind, it's interesting to consider the writing style used on public service websites – plain language, short sentences, and enormous efforts taken for comprehension for all citizens – versus the writing style used in more exploitative products like crypto trading apps, where impenetrable technical terms are used extensively, very little is explained, and the user is enabled to make all kinds of risky trades with minimal safeguards or education.

HOW SCAN READING CAN BE USED TO MANIPULATE PEOPLE

When we read, we don't usually read every word on every page. Not unless we're studying really hard or working our way through something we're enjoying, like a novel for example. Take a look at this:[3]

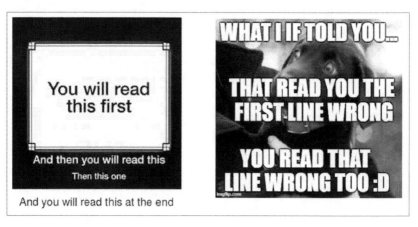

A demonstration of how human visual perception can be manipulated.

On the left, you can see we tend to let visual hierarchy determine the order in which we read things. We've learned it's a good idea to read the big, prominent things first and smaller things later. On the right, you can see how we glance at content and make educated guesses about individual words to save time. This isn't something we're born with. It's a technique called 'scan reading', which we pick up naturally as we get better at reading. Similarly, good writers and page designers learn how to design for scan reading, to help people to do it more efficiently.

Steve Krug published *Don't Make Me Think* in 2000. It's now in its third edition, with over 350,000 copies in print. This book is highly regarded in the UX design industry, as it puts forward a clear explanation for the concept of scan reading by people who are using screens.

Let me show you two more images. The first image explains what we naively might assume is a natural way to read information. In theory, we'd expect readers to take in each successive word, thoroughly paying attention to every element of the design. This naive view of human information-seeking behaviour is similar to the concept of homo economicus from traditional economics – the idea that humans have a limitless supply of attention, energy and critical thinking skills, so we can brute-force our way through any body of content by reading every word on a page in sequence.

A depiction of 'what we design for' in reading behaviour (Krug, 2006)

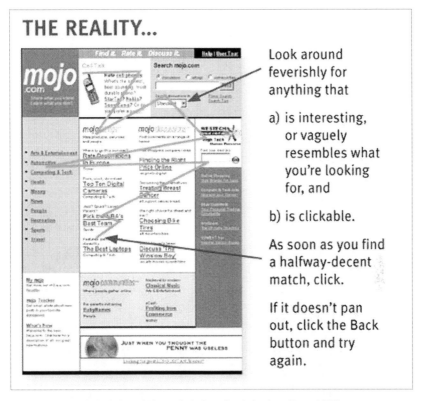

THE REALITY...

A depiction of 'the reality' of reading behaviour (Krug, 2006)

However, Krug argues that while authors might hope that people read every word on every page in a highly attentive and rational manner, the reality is rather different, as shown in the second image (above). In real life, most of us take a 'billboard going by at 60 miles an hour' approach[4] when there's this much information presented to us.[5]

Krug argues that users tend to 'glance at each new page, scan some of the text, and click on the first link that catches their interest or vaguely resembles the thing they're looking for. There are usually large parts of the page that they don't even look at.' He goes on to explain that we've been trained to scan-read from an early age, flicking through newspapers and magazines, for example, or reference books, as we try to narrow down many choices and find just the parts we're interested in.

Other researchers found more evidence. Back in 1997, Morkes and Nielsen did a quantitative empirical study in which 51 participants tested five variations of a website, each one with a different style of writing:[6]

1. A promotional writing style – full of 'marketese'
2. A scannable writing style – intended to encourage scan reading
3. A concise writing style – succinct content
4. An objective writing style – not using promotional language
5. A combined concise, scannable and objective writing style

Each person was given a series of tasks, generally involving looking for the answer to a simple question. The amount of time they took was recorded, as were any errors they made. The findings showed that people performed worse on the promotional style pages, but significantly better with the scannable and concise styles.

This research demonstrated what we might have divined naturally: a writing style has an impact on users' ability to read and understand information. If users read every word on every page in a systematic way, these differences wouldn't have been seen. In a subsequent article, Nielsen (1997) addressed the question, 'How do users read on the web?' with a two-word answer: 'They don't.' He went on: 'People rarely read web pages word by word; instead, they scan the page, picking out individual words and sentences.'[7]

Understanding how people read is vital if you want to design web pages or app screens that work effectively, or – conversely – if you want to create deceptive patterns.

Eye-tracking research is another useful source of insights about reading behaviour. In 2014, Pernice, Whitenton and Nielsen ran an eye tracking study with over 300 participants.[8] In one exercise, people were asked to use a search engine and find some specific information. Eye-tracking technology followed their progress, monitoring how they fixated on the page: 17% of the time, people looked at only one result before clicking onto the next page. They didn't fix their gaze anywhere else. Or, in other words, they picked the first result that seemed 'good enough' to save effort, rather than systematically reading every result on the page. This is a demonstration of an *information foraging strategy*, a technique that was first defined in 1999 by Pirolli and Card, who noticed similarities between animal food foraging strategies and the way in which humans search for information online.[9] When an animal forages for food, it cannot search everywhere or it may die from starvation, so it must use a 'good enough' strategy that provides the most benefit for the lowest cost. Broadly speaking, information foraging can be considered a kind of goal-directed scan-reading strategy.

Generally, scan reading and information foraging can be a pretty effective way of saving ourselves time and energy. But it is only effective in a predictable, trusted environment in which the designer has your best interests in mind. If a designer wants to deceive you, they can take advantage of scan-reading behaviour by hiding pertinent information where you don't expect it, or by using misleading headings and visual hierarchy, among other things.

MISLEADING INFORMATION AND FALSE BELIEFS

If a business publishes misleading information, this can lead users to make decisions that are not in their best interests. This can range from outright lies (fraudulent claims) to ambiguous or manipulative language and design that encourages the user towards a false belief. For example, a business might exploit scan reading by making the headings, links and buttons on a page appear to say one thing, while the body text, if read word-for-word, says another. Similarly, offers can be priced in a manner that requires considerable mental arithmetic and short-term memory to compare properly. If the user is not capable of this task, they might end up with a bad deal that harms them financially. The FTC lists 'false beliefs' as one of the top harms posed to consumers by deceptive patterns[10]. In a 2021 study involving 3,777 participants, researchers Luguri and Strahilevitz found that 'hidden information' doubled the acceptance rates for a product offer, as compared to a neutral design. In other words, participants formed false beliefs about an offer because facts were hidden away from view, and this had a substantial effect on their decisions.[11]

CHAPTER 6
EXPLOITING VULNERABILITIES IN DECISION-MAKING

If you think of the stream of information that enters your mind, you first have to perceive it, and then you have to comprehend it. I've explained how weaknesses in both of these areas can be exploited. After perception and comprehension occur, we then need to engage in critical thinking, or what cognitive psychologists tend to call 'judgement and decision-making' which can also be exploited for commercial gain.[1] To quote whistleblower Christopher Wylie from his book *Mindf*ck*:[2]

'The goal in hacking is to find a weak point in a system and then exploit that vulnerability. In psychological warfare, the weak points are flaws in how people think. If you're trying to hack a person's mind, you need to identify cognitive biases and then exploit them.'

— CHRISTOPHER WYLIE (2020)

A cognitive bias is a mental shortcut that tends to cause a systematic error in judgement and decision-making. Humans fall foul of these biases rather predictably, which led economist Dan Ariely to describe human behaviour as 'predictably irrational'.[3] Despite their shortcomings, cognitive biases are also believed to provide benefits because they provide shortcuts, ways to avoid effortful work in order to save time and energy for other more important matters. Cognitive scientist Aaron Sloman describes this as 'productive laziness' and explains, 'a chess champion who wins by working through all the possible sequences of moves several steps ahead and choosing the optimal one is not as intelligent as the player who avoids explicitly examining so many cases'.[4] Sloman wrote this in 1988 – no doubt he would happily refer to the web instead of chess if he were to write it today. No sensible human would read every result on Google, or every product listing on Amazon before choosing which item to click. Shortcuts are necessary to cope, so today we rely on cognitive biases more than ever, because we simply cannot process all the information we receive in detail.

There are thousands of research papers and well over one hundred types of cognitive biases proposed.[5] Research on cognitive biases started to become well known in the early 2000s, entering the realms of pop psychology, business and design textbooks. The tech industry latched onto this with a great deal of enthusiasm. Some authors were very direct about the purpose of their work. In the introduction of his book *Influence*, Robert Cialdini refers to his area of work as 'the psychology of compliance' (that is, submission to demands of others) and he describes his key principles as 'six universal weapons of influence'.[6] In the book *Hooked*, the author Nir Eyal promotes a 'habit-forming' behavioural model that is nearly identical to Natasha Dow Schüll's model of 'ludic loops' – except Dow Schüll describes her model as 'addiction by design' and presents harrowing accounts of lives destroyed by gambling.[7] Eyal is careful to avoid the word 'addiction', but the connection is obvious.

Today, numerous websites and blogs provide guides on how to exploit cognitive biases for profit; for example, the company Convertize provides a library of cognitive biases that it cheerfully recommends as 'A/B Testing Ideas Based On Neuromarketing', without any mention of negative consequences for the end user, such as being tricked or trapped into unwanted transactions or contracts.[8]

There's also lots of content available about cognitive biases and persuasion that proposes use in a non-exploitative manner – but it's a very short hop from 'use this bias to persuade in a transparent and helpful way' to 'use this bias to see what happens in your next A/B test'. After all, as soon as a design is tested and has statistical evidence proving it to be more profitable than the other designs, it's very likely to be adopted by the business with little further discussion, regardless of whether users truly understand the consequences of their actions.

DEFAULT EFFECT

The default effect is a psychological phenomenon where people tend to stick with the status quo and choose the option presented to them as the default. It's a bias that's been studied in many different contexts, from consumer decisions to public policy. Businesses know that people are more likely to stick with the default option, so they often define the default to be favourable to the business in some way, typically through a preselected checkbox or radio button.

One of the most famous studies on the default effect was carried out by researchers Eric J Johnson and Daniel Goldstein in the 2003 paper 'Do Defaults Save Lives?'.[9] They looked at organ donation consent rates in different countries, and they compared the countries in which users are opted out by default (shown on the left) versus countries in which users are opted in by default (shown on the right).

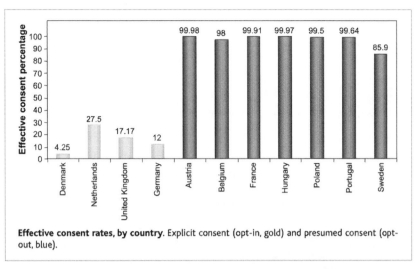

Effective consent rates, by country. Explicit consent (opt-in, gold) and presumed consent (opt-out, blue).

Effective consent rates by country, from Johnson & Goldstein (2003).

As you can see, the difference in consent rates was enormous. A number of things are believed to drive the power of the default effect:

- **Awareness**: for a user to change the default, they first have to become aware that it is possible to do so. (This harks back to the earlier section on exploitation of perceptual vulnerabilities.)
- **Effort**: for the user to change from the default, they have to do something; in this case it involves finding and completing the correct government form. It is possible that citizens might intend to change their choice from the default, but not have time or energy to do so.
- **Authority bias and social proof:** the default effect can be combined with other cognitive biases. For example, the default may be presented as the correct thing to do by a figure of authority (a doctor, for example). Alternatively, it may be portrayed as the thing that everyone else is doing (social proof). These are both known to be powerful cognitive biases in their own right.

In the book *Misbehaving* Richard Thaler did some follow up research, looking at *true* organ donation rates as opposed to *presumed* consent rates.[10] He found that while presuming consent may appear to work on paper, when people die in hospitals the staff will typically ask the family whether the organs should be donated. At that point the presumed consent frequently gets discarded as there is no record of the individual's actual choice. Thaler concluded that 'mandated consent' was a better policy, forcing citizens to make an explicit choice when they renew their driving licence.

The default effect has also been studied in the context of privacy and cookie consent dialogs. A large-scale study conducted by SERNAC, the Chilean consumer protection agency, provides compelling evidence.[11] Over 70,000 participants were presented with different cookie consent interfaces. In one of the interfaces, participants were presented with cookie tracking as opted-in by default, while another presented it as opted-out by default. The opted-out version increased the rate of users rejecting cookies by 86 percentage points.

As you can see from the evidence, the default effect is easy to employ and is very powerful. It is often used by businesses in an exploitative way: to presume user consent for decisions where users might prefer to opt out, if they only knew the true nature of the decision they were being presented with, and were given an explicit choice.

ANCHORING AND FRAMING

The anchoring effect cognitive bias is a psychological phenomenon where individuals rely too heavily on the first piece of information they receive (the anchor) when making decisions. For example, Tversky and Kahneman (1974) conducted a study in which participants were asked to estimate the percentage of African countries in the United Nations.[12] They were first given a random percentage (an anchor), then asked if their estimate would be higher or lower, and then finally asked to provide their estimated figure. The results showed that the estimates of participants were significantly influenced by the anchor they were given: those given a higher anchor estimated a higher number, and those given a lower anchor estimated a lower number. This insight is frequently used by marketers in an exploitative manner when pricing consumer products – for example, where an initial price is created to be artificially high so that a discount can be presented, giving a sense of value for money.

Framing is a similar cognitive bias where individuals rely too heavily on the way information is presented rather than on the underlying facts. In 1981, Tversky and Kahneman carried out an experiment in which they gave participants a scenario relating to a hypothetical disease, and were given two treatment programmes to choose from.[13] Depending on their experimental group, the outcomes of the treatment programmes were framed either positively: 'X people will be saved'; or negatively: 'Y people will die'. They found that the framing had a pronounced effect on participants' choices, even though the underlying facts were identical in both cases.

In the book *Predictably Irrational*, Dan Ariely reported a study that demonstrates the manipulative power of this type of cognitive bias.[14] He created two different fictional designs of *The Economist* magazine's subscription page, and presented them to 200 students (100 per design), asking them to pick their preferred subscription type. Unknown to the participants, one of the designs contained a trick (design A, below), intended to get participants to perceive the combined print and web subscription as better value. It involved providing an extra 'decoy' subscription: the print magazine on its own for the same price as the print and web subscription. As you can see in the figure below, the presence of the decoy print subscription in design A caused the print and web subscription to be selected much more frequently (84% selected) than when it was omitted in design B (32% selected).

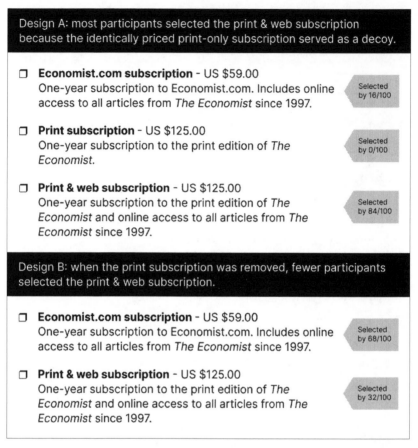

Design A: most participants selected the print & web subscription because the identically priced print-only subscription served as a decoy.

☐ **Economist.com subscription** - US $59.00
One-year subscription to Economist.com. Includes online access to all articles from *The Economist* since 1997.

Selected by 16/100

☐ **Print subscription** - US $125.00
One-year subscription to the print edition of *The Economist.*

Selected by 0/100

☐ **Print & web subscription** - US $125.00
One-year subscription to the print edition of *The Economist* and online access to all articles from *The Economist* since 1997.

Selected by 84/100

Design B: when the print subscription was removed, fewer participants selected the print & web subscription.

☐ **Economist.com subscription** - US $59.00
One-year subscription to Economist.com. Includes online access to all articles from *The Economist* since 1997.

Selected by 68/100

☐ **Print & web subscription** - US $125.00
One-year subscription to the print edition of *The Economist* and online access to all articles from *The Economist* since 1997.

Selected by 32/100

Dan Ariely's Economist magazine study, where the presence of a decoy option influenced participants' decision-making.

SOCIAL PROOF

The social proof cognitive bias is a phenomenon in which individuals are likely to conform to the behaviour of others. It's also known as the 'bandwagon effect', 'groupthink' or the 'herd effect'. To put it another way, if we see that numerous other people perceive something as valuable, we are likely to believe that they are correct. This is a shortcut that allows us to avoid the hard work of carrying out a critical evaluation of our own.

In 2014, a group of researchers working with HMRC tested the impact of social proof in a large-scale experiment.[15] They designed five different tax bill reminder letters, each with a different message, shown in the table below. They sent these letters to a random selection of 100,000 UK taxpayers, and tracked the response rate (which they measured as a successful payment of the tax bill within 23 days).

No.	Message	Response rate
1	"Nine out of ten people pay their tax on time"	1.30%
2	"Nine out of ten people in the UK pay their tax on time"	2.10%
3	"Nine out of ten people in the UK pay their tax on time. You are currently in the very small minority of people who have not paid us yet"	5.10%
4	"Paying tax means we all gain from vital public services like the NHS, roads, and schools"	1.60%
5	"Not paying tax means we all lose out on vital public services like the NHS, roads, and schools"	1.60%

Findings from HMRC tax letter study (Hallsworth et al., 2017).

As you can see, messages 1, 2 and 3 used different styles of social proof, while messages 4 and 5 did not. Message 3 employed the most aggressive social proof phrasing and it was by far the best performing. This was a big win for HMRC, and timely tax payments benefit the country as a whole. Of course, there's nothing exploitative about this example – accurate and true social proof information is constructive and helpful. However, it can become exploitative when the information is tampered with in some way, and the user is purposefully not informed about what's going on.

Online, social proof is typically presented as reviews, case studies, testimonials and data (ratings or 'likes'). For example, consider a testimonial. If it is completely fabricated by the company, then that's just false advertising – fraud, plain and simple. Similarly, if it's provided by a real user but they were paid to write something positive, then that's fraudulent too.

But what if it's real, and the user was paid to give an honest and unbiased review? Incentivisation creates a grey area in which exploitative practices can be hidden. For example, what kind of payment was the reviewer given? Was the payment proportional to the service provided? Did the company imply that future employment as a reviewer might be conditional on a positive review this time? Did the reviewer give a positive review because of the incentive, even though they were not asked to? We all know from personal experience that if we receive a gift or a big discount we will be less critical of its short-comings than if we had paid for it ourselves at full price. So, incentivised reviews should always be labelled with a disclosure – the user needs to be told that the review was paid for. However, the problem with disclosures is that they can be ambiguous. Take this Amazon UK review for an airfryer:[16]

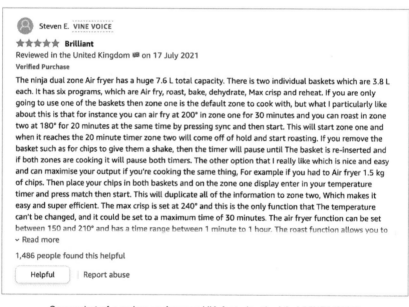

Screenshot of a review on Amazon UK, featuring the label 'VINE VOICE'

Next to the reviewer's name is the label 'VINE VOICE'. The user cannot click the label or hover over the label to reveal more information – and it's not explained on the page. If the user searches for 'vine voice' in the product search box at the top of the page, nothing relevant appears in the search results. Buried deep in the Amazon UK website is a 'help library'. From there, the user can search for 'vine voice' and find an explanation: that reviews with this label are paid reviews, because the reviewers were given the products for free. This is quite evidently not an adequate disclosure.

There are other ways that social proof can be manipulated. In the early days of the mobile app stores, a company called Appsfire pioneered a clever approach in a product for app developers called AppBooster.[17] It involved showing users a 'fake' review page in which a rating and review were requested. If users gave a thumbs up with their review, they were asked to submit it to the App Store. If users gave a thumbs down their review was transferred into an email support thread hidden away from the public – although none of this was explained to the user. You can see the steps below.

The AppBooster 'thumbs up' user experience

The AppBooster 'thumbs down' user experience

As you can see, AppBooster was dishonest about the true purpose of the 'thumbs up' and 'thumbs down' buttons. A more honest approach would be to let users decide for themselves whether they want to leave a public App Store review or email the developer privately.

Today, this sort of manipulative technique is forbidden in the Apple and Google app stores, so it's not seen so often. Other approaches to manipulating social proof include delaying the publication of negative reviews (holding them in a queue longer than positive reviews), or simply showing them less prominently.

SCARCITY EFFECT

Scarcity is a cognitive bias that describes the tendency for people to place greater value on resources they believe to be in limited supply. It typically influences decision-making by increasing impulsiveness and risk-taking, as people feel a sense of urgency to acquire the resource before it runs out.

One of the first and most famous studies on scarcity involves cookies – the delicious baked kind, not browser cookies. In 1975, researchers Worchel, Lee and Adwole recruited 146 undergraduate students and carried out a series of experiments.[18] Participants were shown a jar of either ten cookies or two cookies, and were asked to rate how much they wanted to eat them. The results showed that participants in the two-cookie condition rated the cookies as *more desirable* and *more attractive* compared to those in the ten-cookie condition.

Then, to make matters more exciting, the researchers engaged in some theatrics during the experiment. An actor entered the room with another jar of either two or ten cookies. The actor explained that they needed to swap their jar with the one the participant was already looking at. This served to draw attention to the difference in the number of cookies, before and after. In the conditions where the number of cookies was reduced, participants rated those cookies as *even more attractive*. This just goes to show that scarcity is effective, and the effectiveness is intensified when a person's attention is drawn to the scarcity.

In the real world, scarcity is a fact of life, and it can be very helpful to provide scarcity information to users. For example, if a user has specific dates they need to take as annual leave, it is important for them to know if their desired travel tickets are close to selling out; if they are, they'd better book them immediately or they'll miss their chance.

While honest and true messages are entirely acceptable, the scarcity effect is so powerful that it leads businesses to create fake scarcity, or to manipulate the concept of scarcity using ambiguous language, categories and user interfaces. We'll look into this further in part 3 of the book, on types of deceptive pattern.

SUNK COST FALLACY

The sunk cost fallacy is a phenomenon where individuals continue investing resources in an endeavour simply because they have already 'sunk' a significant amount of effort or resources in it. Research conducted by Arkes and Blumer in 1985 showed that individuals are more likely to persist in a task when they have invested in it, even if the investment is irretrievable and continuing the task is not rational.[19] In one experiment, they gave 61 participants the following scenario. Before reading beyond the excerpt below, consider how you'd respond to this scenario.

> Assume that you have spent $100 on a ticket for a weekend ski trip to Michigan. Several weeks later you buy a $50 ticket for a weekend ski trip to Wisconsin. You think you will enjoy the Wisconsin ski trip more than the Michigan ski trip. As you are putting your just-purchased Wisconsin ski trip ticket in your wallet, you notice that the Michigan ski trip and the Wisconsin ski trip are for the same weekend! It's too late to sell either ticket, and you cannot return either one. You must use one ticket and not the other. Which ski trip will you go on?

Given the fact that all the money is now spent and cannot be retrieved, it would be irrational for you to consider the cost of the trips in making a choice. You've already worked out that you'll enjoy the Wisconsin trip so the logical choice would be Wisconsin. But did the participants in the study all pick that option? No. In fact only 46% of the respondents did. The sunk cost of the Michigan trip influenced the majority of respondents (54%).

The sunk cost fallacy is often employed in deceptive patterns by drawing users in with an attractive offer, using up their time, attention and energy going through a long-winded series of steps only to finally reveal the truth that the offer is less attractive than initially stated: the price is higher, for instance, or the terms less favourable. This will be explained further in part 3.

RECIPROCITY BIAS

The reciprocity cognitive bias is a phenomenon in which people tend to feel obligated to return favours to others after they have been given something. It is sometimes believed to be a form of social currency, as people may feel obligated to respond to a favour with a favour of their own. In 2013, the UK government ran a large A/B test with over 1 million website visitors, in which they tested eight different designs.[20] When people had finished renewing their vehicle tax on the *gov.uk* website, they were taken to a variant of this page:

A variant of the UK government vehicle tax completion page, as used in an A/B test.

They tested eight different variants of this page. The one you can see above is the control (1) and the most effective variant (7) is shown below. The two pages are identical, apart from the message in the version below: 'If you needed an organ transplant would you have one? If so please help others.'

Another variant of the UK government vehicle tax completion page, featuring a persuasive element regarding the NHS Organ Donor Register.

You might expect the effect to be small, because the text looks so unremarkable – but you'd be wrong. With the first design (1), 2.3% of people went on to register as organ donors. With the second design (7), 3.2% went on to register as organ donors. That's one percentage point higher – or to put it another way, about *one-third bigger* than the control condition.

In its report, the BIT (the UK government's Behavioural Insights Team) refer to this design as tapping into the 'reciprocity' bias.[21] In this case, it is applied in an honest and transparent manner, but it would be deceptive if it were based on lies or misleading statements, and it's easy to imagine it being used for nefarious ends.

CHAPTER 7
EXPLOITING
EXPECTATIONS

Everyone has expectations of websites and apps. Helpful designers play into those expectations by employing guidelines, user-centred patterns and design systems to make sure their products are consistent and predictable, so users don't have to relearn how to use the product every time they do something new.[1]

In a 2016 study, researchers Nikolaus and Bonhert gave 135 participants a grid and asked them to specify the expected location of common website elements like the logo, search and advertisements.[2] They compared the aggregated user expectations against fifty real website layouts. In the figure below, you can see how users generally expected the search feature to be near the top right of the page, while the real position of the search feature was also generally at the top right. This just goes to show that users usually know what to expect, and that designers usually know that it's helpful to support those expectations.

User expectation of the position of the search feature on websites (left) and real position of search (right). From Nikolaus and Bonhert, 2016.

An exploitative designer can take their knowledge of user expectations and treat it as a weakness to be exploited for profit. The most famous example of this is probably from the game Flappy Bird that soared to the top of the iOS app store rankings out of nowhere in 2013. At the time, the app store ranking algorithm boosted games to the top if they had frequent positive reviews, among other factors. The game involved a compelling loop of dying and retrying levels, and it employed a trivially simple deceptive pattern to generate more reviews: when retrying, the 'play' button was replaced by a 'rate' button, in the same screen location, size and visual style. This was frequently clicked accidentally by users who were seeking to retry the level, and they were taken into a page of the App Store inviting them to leave a review. Of course, this deceptive pattern was greatly supported by the fact that the game was fun, so most users were happy to leave a positive review, even though they'd arrived at the review page unintentionally. At one point, the game achieved over 700,000 US reviews in a month, more than a top-ranking game would normally receive in a year.

This specific type of deceptive pattern has been called 'the fast forward trick'[3] and 'affirmative tunnelling',[4] though there are many other types of deceptive patterns that fall under the general strategy of exploiting user expectations, as we'll see in subsequent chapters. It is most commonly referred to as 'misdirection', where the user is led to expect something they desire to happen, yet something else undesirable happens instead.

CHAPTER 8
RESOURCE DEPLETION AND PRESSURE

Everyone has a finite amount of time – we all die eventually. To add to this, we're all generally rather busy while we're alive: we spend most of our time working, sleeping and completing tasks that we don't really want to, like tidying our bedrooms and filling in forms. We also have a limited amount of energy each day before the burden of *cognitive load*[1] or *cognitive friction*[2] makes us fatigued. When we get tired, we become less able to engage in difficult cognitive tasks, more likely to use shortcuts (cognitive biases) and more error prone.[3]

This simple insight can be used in an exploitative manner to wear us down and trip us up. Software doesn't need food, sleep or rest. A tedious series of steps will not bother an inanimate piece of software, but it will bother the user on the receiving end. This means that making something difficult is an effective way of stopping people from doing costly things – like cancelling subscriptions, opting out of surveillance tracking or exporting data. The strategy of exploitative resource depletion is often called 'sludge'.[4] Cass Sunstein explains the problem of sludge in his book on the topic:

'In all likelihood, your life has been made worse because of sludge
—a 'viscous mixture,' consisting of frictions that prevent you from

doing what you want to do or from going where you want to go. [...] In many cases, sludge imposes economic harm. [...] It hurts patients, parents, teachers, doctors, nurses, employees, customers, investors, and developers. It compromises fundamental rights, including the right to vote and the right to be free from discrimination on the basis of race and sex. It is a pervasive source of inequality. Sludge can also be an assault on human dignity. [...] Kafka captures that; his novels depict a world in which people cannot navigate life or escape their predicament because of that viscous mixture. [...] It hurts all of us, but if you are sick, old, disabled, or poor, or if you don't have a lot of education, sludge is a curse.'

— CASS SUNSTEIN, 2022

In deceptive patterns literature, exploitative sludge in the interface is typically referred to as 'obstruction'[5] or in some cases 'roach motel',[6] but we'll come to that later.

It's easy to create sludge. A business can add lots of steps and interruptions to any process. They can make the user fill in long forms, and enter their password multiple times. If they want to go really far, they can force people to send a letter by post, compel them to go somewhere in person, or make them use a call centre that has a confusing menu and long call-waiting times. This tactic is common with newspaper subscriptions and gym memberships. Life is full of interruptions and competing priorities, which means that sludge can make subscriptions last a little longer than users intend, which counts as free revenue for the business.

The impact of just one extra step can be substantial. In one study, BIT worked with HMRC to send letters to thousands of British citizens, asking them to pay their tax bills. They sent two different letters. In the first letter, they pointed users to a webpage that required users to click a link to get to the tax payment form (an extra step); in the second, they pointed users to the tax payment form directly, with no extra step.

The impact of the extra step was notable, with 5.1 percentage points fewer people completing the task.[7] It's easy to imagine the impact of adding numerous extra steps, tiring users out and making them give up before reaching their goals.

As well as sludge, there are other forms of resource depletion that businesses can employ. A common technique is to impose a deadline so instead of wasting a user's precious time, they create an artificial limit on it. Things like time-limited offers and countdown timers in checkouts prevent users from believing that they have the time to engage in careful evaluation and calculated decision-making (also known as 'pressure selling', and the 'urgency' and 'scarcity' deceptive patterns). While these techniques often elicit an emotional response (fear, stress, and so on), they also have the practical impact of forcing even the most level-headed users to make decisions more quickly, which may lead them to use shortcuts, like: 'I don't have time to read all of this but the positive reviews probably mean it's safe' (social proof bias); or 'I don't have time to weigh up my options, so I'll pick the middle tier since it's a bit less expensive' (anchoring and framing bias), and so on.

Nagging is another technique that falls into the broad category of resource depletion. Every time an app or a website asks you for permission to do something, you have to spend your limited time and attention responding. It's like a time and attention tax that businesses impose on users who do not want to comply with the business's wishes. Although the cost is non-financial, it still adds up and eventually becomes non-trivial, at which point you may decide that it's more cost efficient to just give in and agree to whatever the business is asking for.

It's also important to recognise that some groups in society have less free time than others. People who are on the poverty line are more likely to work multiple jobs for long hours, have exhausting commutes and difficult home life situations. When our resources are depleted and we are tired, we are vulnerable to being tricked and trapped by businesses who wish to profit from us.

CHAPTER 9
FORCING AND BLOCKING

Forcing typically involves putting a mandatory step in front of the action the user wants to complete, which they cannot decline. Blocking involves preventing the user from doing the thing they want to do. For example, if a user wants to export their data, the business prevents it by simply not offering this feature, or mentioning it anywhere. In turn this locks in the user, and makes it impossible for them to leave without saying goodbye to their data.

Perhaps some of the most famous examples of forcing and blocking are in the use of coffee pod machines and printer ink.

Coffee machine manufacturer Keurig is well known for its K-Cup pod machines that require the user to insert a specially designed 'brew pod' for every cup of coffee they make. After being on the market for a while, some competitors created copies of the Keurig pods, allowing consumers to choose who to buy their coffee from. This bothered Keurig, as it was eating into its profits; their business model was to sell the machine at a relatively low price, and then to lock in consumers, making long-term profit from them as they were forced to buy all their coffee from Keurig. In 2015, Keurig's response to this was to add digital rights management (DRM) to their pods and machines. This involved putting radio-frequency identification (RFID) chips on every

pod, so that the machine could check whether the pod was manufactured by Keurig or by a competitor.

Amusingly, this backfired as customers created YouTube videos and
guides showing how to circumvent the DRM – all you needed to do
was cut the RFID chip off an old pod and place it onto the sensor of
your machine[1].

More recently, printer manufacturer HP Inc. has been engaging in very
similar tricks.[2] In March 2023, many HP customers woke up one
morning to find that HP had hobbled the functionality of their printers
via a cloud update, so they no longer accepted third-party ink
cartridges. This meant that some printers simply stopped working
overnight, even though they were working fine and were full of ink –
the only problem was that they contained ink cartridges manufactured
by a competitor.

In the world of interface design and software, it's even easier to add
forcing and blocking functions as it takes very little effort to create and
rearrange pages. We'll cover this in part 3 on types of deceptive
pattern.

CHAPTER 10
EXPLOITING EMOTIONAL VULNERABILITIES

Humans do not like to experience uncomfortable emotions like guilt, shame, fear or regret, and will often make decisions to avoid those emotions. This can be applied in an exploitative way to steer users into, or away from, certain decisions. This has been employed for many years in print and TV advertising, and psychological research has shown it to be effective.

For example, Krishen and Bui (2015) recruited 122 participants, showed them an advertisement relating to obesity and had them complete a survey involving hypothetical scenarios and attitudes, including the intention to subsequently consume an indulgent dessert.[1] Two advertisements were used: one with a message about *fear* (top image), and another with a message about *hope* (bottom image).[2]

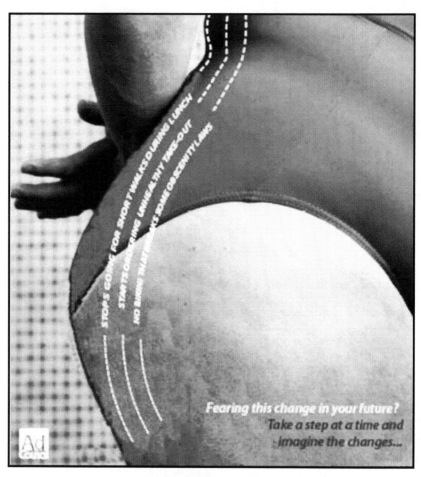

'Fearing this change in your future?' – advertisement used in an experiment by Krishen and Bui (2015).

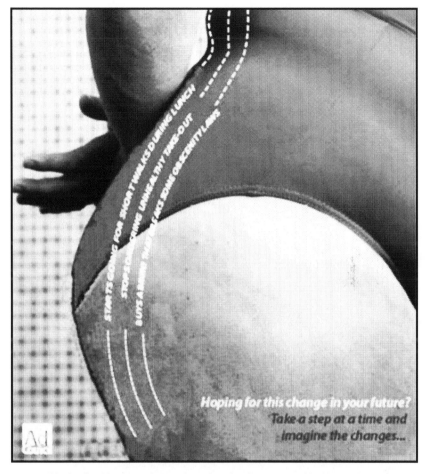

'Hoping for this change in your future' – advertisement used in an experiment by Krishen and Bui (2015).

The researchers found that the fear-based advertisement was significantly more effective than the hope-based advertisement in encouraging the intention to abstain from consuming an indulgent dessert. Today, fear is commonly used to elicit behaviour in public health campaigns, and the ethics of this tactic is debated.[3] Emotions are also widely employed to manipulate users of apps and websites, which we'll cover in part 3.

CHAPTER 11
EXPLOITING ADDICTION

Consider some of the following criteria against your own behaviour, and your friends and family:

1. Using something for longer than you intended.
2. Trying to cut down, but not quite managing it.
3. Usage requires you to spend a lot of time recovering (from sleep deprivation, for instance).
4. Feeling cravings when you're not using it.
5. Usage causing you to fail to fulfil your obligations (at work, school or home, and so on).
6. Continuing to use it even though it interferes with your relationships (for example, recurring arguments with or resentment towards your partner).
7. Using it in hazardous situations (such as while driving).
8. Choosing not to attend social or recreational events so you can use it instead.
9. Feeling withdrawal symptoms when you can't use it.

This list is paraphrased from the DSM-5, the book used by US psychiatrists to diagnose mental health disorders – in this case, substance abuse disorder.[1] But it's easy to look at this list and think about compulsive behaviours in games and other digital products. It must look familiar if you know someone who has developed an unhealthy habit with League of Legends, Call of Duty, Twitter, Facebook or whatever else. This is known as *behavioural addiction* – where there are no drugs involved – but the phenomena are very similar.[2]

In fact, some neuroscientists claim they have found evidence that *all* addictions share the same biological origins in the human brain.[3] Whether you're abusing a drug or just can't stop playing League of Legends, they argue that it's the brain's reward system that's being tapped into – specifically, the mesolimbic dopamine pathway.[4]

It's easy to exploit addiction for profit if you're willing to overlook the negative impacts. Some products are designed from the ground up to be as addictive as possible, and they use various forms of manipulation and deception to do this. To quote the first president of Facebook, Sean Parker:[5]

> How do we consume as much of your time and conscious attention as possible? [...] we needed to sort of give you a little dopamine hit every once in a while because someone liked or commented on a photo or a post or whatever... It's a social validation feedback loop... You're exploiting a vulnerability in human psychology... [The inventors] understood this, consciously, and we did it anyway.
>
> — SEAN PARKER, 2017

Surprisingly, one of the most effective ways to make something addictive is to design it so that recipients *don't always get what they want,* and to only let them get it in an unpredictable way. This is called a 'variable reward schedule' or 'intermittent reinforcement schedule'.

This was famously demonstrated by psychologist BF Skinner in 1938.[6] He conducted experiments with rats and pigeons in which he presented them with a lever to press. When the animal pressed the lever, they received a food pellet or some other reward. Skinner discovered that when the reward was given on a variable schedule (that is, in an unpredictable way), the animals were more likely to keep pressing the lever than when the reward was given on a fixed schedule (in a predictable way). This is best understood in the context of the dopamine cycle, shown below.[7]

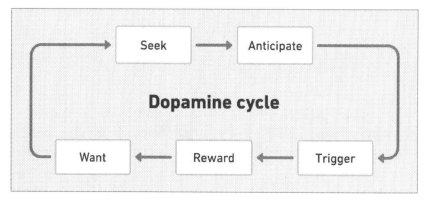

Simplified diagram of the dopamine cycle

It's believed that the variable schedule works because the animals *never know when the next reward is coming.* This creates a sense of excitement and anticipation that keeps them engaged in the behaviour for longer periods of time, which is now understood to relate to the dopamine cycle (shown above). A predictable schedule breaks the cycle because it doesn't give this sense of excitement and anticipation. Given how profitable addiction can be, it is very common to see addiction models being recommended as good practice in marketing and product design literature, even though the harms to society are well known. Eyal and Hoover's 'hook model' (2014) is perhaps one of the most famous examples, though if you look at it closely you'll see that it's really just a rebranded version of the dopamine cycle.[8] Instead of addiction, it's 'hooked', which appears to be an effort to make the exploitation of addiction more socially acceptable.

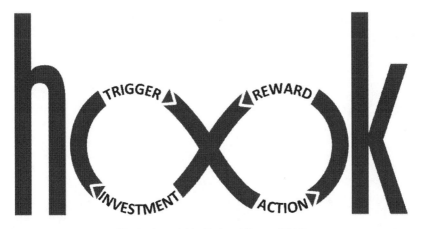

The hook model by Eyal and Hoover (2014).

Behavioural addiction is often associated with the user going into 'the zone', a state of flow where they lose track of time and their worldly concerns, becoming deeply immersed in the activity. Anthropologist Natasha Dow Schüll argues that it's the zone that many people seek when they become addicted to gambling, as it gives them an escape from their day to day problems.[9]

It is possible to exploit this insight by designing products to avoid interrupting users when they are in the zone. For example, infinite scroll is employed in most social media products, and it serves to avoid interrupting users with pagination buttons, nor reminding them with how many pages of content they have browsed through. The inventor of infinite scrolling, Aza Raskin, regrets creating it. In a 2019 interview he said, 'I regret that I didn't think more about how this thing would be used [...] I know as a designer that by taking away the stopping cue, I can make you do what I want you to do.'[10]

Autoplay is another feature that works in a similar way. When the user finishes streaming a video, another video is automatically selected and played without the user needing to take an action, which can lead to them spending more time than they intended using the product. Similarly, notifications and gamification features (like streaks) can be used to drive users back into a product. When combined with a compulsion loop, this creates a potent mix. Together, these features have drawn much concern, leading to proposals for regulation, such as the proposed US Social Media Addiction Reduction Technology (SMART) Act.[11]

Video games are one of the biggest areas of tech that exploit the principles of addiction for profit. One of the most controversial techniques is the 'loot box': a device that uses a random number generator in order to let users purchase the chance to win virtual items that offer a gameplay advantage or social status within the game world. This is essentially a form of gambling, addictive because of the variable reward schedule which taps into the dopamine cycle, as described earlier. This has led numerous experts to call for it to be regulated more extensively.[12]

But how did we get here? Up until the 1990s, the normal revenue model for video games was pretty simple: money was made when the game was purchased in a shop. This meant that the strategy for success involved maximising gameplay quality and using traditional marketing to increase sales.

In those days, loot boxes were included in many games but without any sort of revenue model attached. For example, if you play the 1996 Nintendo racing game Mario Kart, you'll find that if you drive over an item box, you'll pick up an unknown item. This ranges from low value, such as a banana (with a bit of skill you can throw this in front of a competitor and cause them to spin off the race track), to high value, such as a star, which gives you invulnerability to all obstacles. What's interesting is that the game designers tweaked the item box algorithm so that it was not truly random; instead, they designed it to be very kind and player friendly. If you were in first place of the race, you were more likely to receive a low-value item, and if you were near the back, you were more likely to receive a high-value item. This served to balance the gameplay experience – it stopped novice players from being left too far behind, and it stopped good players from getting too far ahead, so a very mixed group of people (for example, parents and kids) could play together and still enjoy the thrill of a competitive race. In those days, gameplay was primarily optimised for maximum fun.

The advent of the web, mobile apps and integrated payment systems brought about a new revenue model involving in-game purchases and microtransactions, leading gameplay to be optimised for maximum profit. This rapidly became a dominant force in the gaming industry, and it opened the door to predatory practices and deceptive patterns. Game designers started to spend a lot more effort optimising their game algorithms to create a compulsion loop (so people kept playing) and to drive in-game purchases. When combined with paid loot boxes, this became known as 'gamblification'.[13]

In 2017, game designer Manveer Heir was interviewed about the use of these practices by his former employer EA (Electronic Arts), one of the largest game producers in the world.[14] He said about microtransactions and loot boxes:

'It's the same reason we added card packs to Mass Effect 3: how do you get people to keep coming back to a thing instead of "just" playing for 60 to 100 hours? [...] EA and those big publishers in general only care about the highest return on investment. [...] They don't actually care about what the players want, they care about what the players will pay for. You need to understand the amount of money that's at play with microtransactions. . . . I've seen people literally spend $15,000 on Mass Effect multiplayer cards.'

– GAME DESIGNER MANVEER HEIR (2017)

Loot boxes are becoming increasingly regulated. Games in the Apple App Store[15] or Google Play[16] are now required to disclose the odds of winning in a loot box interaction; and in 2018, the Belgian Gambling Commission banned loot boxes for any businesses that do not have gambling licences, though this has been criticised as being weakly enforced.[17]

Even without loot boxes, game designers can find many ways to create recurrent consumer spending hooks.[18] For example, a game can be designed to be fun at the start, but then it can become very hard work (aka a grind) or very difficult. From that point, the user can be offered the means to 'pay to skip' the hard work, or 'pay to win' and get past a difficult part of the game.[19] When deeply involved in a game, players can find themselves getting carried away and spending large amounts of money, owing to the carefully designed compulsion loops and deceptive patterns. Manipulation, deception and addiction in game design is a thriving area of research, and if you wish to read more, good starting points are the report 'Insert Coin' by the Norwegian Consumer Council[20] and 'When the Cat's Away' (2021) by Scott Goodstein.[21]

CHAPTER 12
DRAWING A LINE BETWEEN PERSUASION AND MANIPULATION

I'm often asked by designers if there's an easy way to distinguish between exploitative practices and honest persuasion. Is there a line we can mark with police tape like in a movie? 'Do not cross! All designs beyond this point are deceptive or manipulative!'

Unfortunately, it's all quite complicated. If you're looking for an easy answer, it's probably a good idea to just avoid creating anything that looks similar to the patterns described in the book, and to find out what the law is in your jurisdiction. Another approach is to look at the outcome of harm. If a design creates negative consequences for users, this is a problem and you can work backwards from there, investigating the causes. This perspective is practical for enforcers and investigators, but it's not so useful for designers who want to do the right thing before any harm occurs.

Direct deception is relatively easy to characterise. If a design contains an outright lie – a false claim that's just not true – that's deception, plain and simple. So there's one line you quite obviously shouldn't cross, and unless you live on the moon you probably have some very long-standing consumer laws in your jurisdiction that forbid this. But there's another type of deception, known as 'indirect deception', which occurs when a design misleads users into holding false beliefs without explicitly lying to them (perhaps by omitting pertinent information or by using ambiguous language). Most deceptive patterns are like this. Indirect deception is not as easy to draw a line around – some examples are worse than others so there's a whole range of severity to consider. Then you've also got the broader concept of manipulation; it's possible for a design to influence or coerce a user without deceiving them. For example, if you use harsh emotional manipulation to steer the user into making a certain choice, you're coercing them, and you may be leading to an outcome of harm – yet it's not deception.[1]

If we zoom out into the world of philosophy and ethics, we'll start to see how complicated it gets. In the 2015 paper 'Fifty Shades of Manipulation', Cass Sunstein gives an analysis of this.[2] In his words:

'an action does not count as manipulative merely because it is an effort to alter people's behavior. If you are a passenger in a car, and you warn the driver that he is about to get into a crash, you are not engaged in manipulation. The same is true if you remind someone that a bill is due. A calorie label and an energy efficiency label are not ordinarily counted as forms of manipulation. So long as a private or public institution is informing people, or "just providing the facts," it is hard to complain of manipulation. There is also a large difference between persuading people and manipulating them. With (non-manipulative) persuasion, people are given facts and reasons, presented in a sufficiently fair and neutral way; manipulation is something different. It is often thought that when people are being manipulated, they are treated as "puppets on a string." Almost no one wants to be someone else's puppet (at least without consent), [...] the idea of "manipulation" can be applied to many kinds of behavior; but it is not entirely clear that it is a unitary concept, or that we can identify necessary and sufficient conditions. Manipulation takes multiple forms. It has at least fifty shades, and some people wonder if they are tightly identified with one another.'

Sunstein goes on to argue that the problem is multidimensional, in the sense that there's a few different things we need to consider at once. He explains that explicit user consent can make manipulation more acceptable (e.g. 'Help me give up smoking. You have my permission to try anything!'). He also explains that transparency can help too – if you clearly inform the user that you are trying to persuade them in a certain way towards a certain outcome, this reduces the possibility of being covert.

In summary, it turns out that there is no single line that we can mark as 'do not cross'. If the world of persuasion, manipulation and deception was a planet, it's perhaps more accurate to say that we know there are some territories we shouldn't go into at all, and other territories that bring varying levels of risk of something harmful or illegal.

I prefer to keep things simple, though. If you work with digital products, here's my advice for you: don't use false claims and know your local laws. Steer well clear of anything that looks like the deceptive or manipulative patterns detailed in this book. Be mindful that good intentions don't absolve you from the responsibility of preventing outcomes of harm, so you should carry out research to anticipate and map these potential outcomes. If you find negative outcomes, make changes to prevent them. If you do that, you're probably doing a good job and you can let the philosophers, ethicists and legislators worry about the bigger picture.

PART THREE
TYPES OF DECEPTIVE PATTERN

When I created *darkpatterns.org* in 2010, my objective was to spread awareness, so a large part of my focus was on branding and promotion. The names I chose were intended to be intriguing and memorable, so the world would find out about them. As a result, I didn't create a rigorous classification system. It was more of a rallying cry to action.

If you review the literature on deceptive patterns today, you'll find a somewhat bewildering array of different taxonomies and naming schemes. They're all useful in one way or another, though the earlier work tends to be more primitive, and the later work tends to be more sophisticated owing to the larger body of evidence and knowledge available to draw on.

Different taxonomies typically have different objectives and tend to come from different areas of expertise. Behavioural economists and HCI researchers generally use psychological principles in their taxonomies. Mathur et al., for example, connect most of their deceptive design patterns with a specific cognitive bias. Similarly, Gray et al. (2018) based their work on a body of literature associated with UX and UI design, so their taxonomy had a strong UX/UI focus.[1]

More recently, deceptive patterns have become an area of interest for legal scholars, legislators and regulators. They tend to frame their taxonomies around the laws and legal terminology that's relevant to their subject matter and their local jurisdiction. For example, the European Data Protection Board (EDPB) created a taxonomy that's focused on privacy in social media platforms in the EU, drawing connections to the rules in the GDPR.[2] This is useful if you happen to work in that area, but not quite so useful elsewhere.

The point here is that different taxonomies serve different purposes. You need to know what they are for before you critique them or use them in your work. If you're seeking an overarching analysis of different taxonomies, you can take a look at the OECD's 2022 'Dark Commercial Patterns' report (Annex B)[3] or Mathur, Mayer and Kshirsagar's 2021 research paper, 'What Makes a Dark Pattern... Dark?'[4]

CHAPTER 13
INTRODUCING THE MATHUR ET AL. TAXONOMY

The taxonomy I prefer to use in my work as an expert witness is the Mathur et al. taxonomy (2019) because it is practical to use and strongly evidence-based. It was created by a group of seven researchers at Princeton University and the University of Chicago and was published in the paper, 'Dark Patterns at Scale: Findings from a Crawl of 11K Shopping Websites'.[1] In their research, the team used a machine-learning algorithm to analyse about 53,000 product pages on 11,000 websites, which revealed 1,818 instances of deceptive patterns. They then took these instances and analysed them in detail, which led to a taxonomy, shown in the list below. This taxonomy is mainly aimed at eCommerce, but it provides some broad categories that can be applied to almost any area of user experience, making it quite flexible.

You'll notice that I am not proposing a new taxonomy based on the exploitative strategies that we covered earlier. This is because deceptive patterns usually don't fit tidily under one exploitative strategy or another – they tend to be creatively combined in different ways. For example, a deceptive pattern like 'trick wording' as executed on a specific website might take advantage of 'exploitation of expectations' and 'manipulation of comprehension' together at once, while another designer might do it differently on another website.

When considering a taxonomy of deceptive patterns, it's tempting to view them as prescriptive – that there are a certain number of types that can be implemented. In reality, there's no limit to human ingenuity and exploitative behaviour. Even good practice guidelines can be used as inspiration for deceptive patterns, as they can be flipped from something helpful into something harmful.[2] Deceptive patterns are often created in an opportunistic and pragmatic manner: if something works, the business doesn't need to stop and carefully consider the exact reasons why. Think of it like a brawl in a kung fu movie. If a character sees a nearby prop – whether it's an umbrella, a ladder or a mop – they'll pick it up and give it a go. If it doesn't work, they'll move on quickly to something else, because results matter more than principles. Everyone tries different patterns in different ways.

I hope I've now explained why the landscape of deceptive patterns is so messy, and how taxonomies are always going to have some limitations. That said, taxonomies are useful analytical tools so long as you remember that the map is not the territory. With that in mind, here's the Mathur et al. taxonomy, as put forward in their 2019 paper 'Dark Patterns at Scale'.[3]

SNEAKING

- **Sneak into Basket:** Adding additional products to users' shopping carts without their consent.
- **Hidden Costs:** Revealing previously undisclosed charges to users right before they make a purchase.
- **Hidden Subscription:** Charging users a recurring fee under the pretence of a one-time fee or a free trial.

URGENCY

- **Countdown Timer:** Indicating to users that a deal or discount will expire using a counting-down timer.
- **Limited-time Message:** Indicating to users that a deal or sale will expire soon without specifying a deadline.

MISDIRECTION

- **Confirmshaming**: Using language and emotion (shame) to steer users away from making a certain choice.
- **Visual Interference**: Using style and visual presentation to steer users to or away from certain choices.
- **Trick Wording**: Using confusing language to steer users into making certain choices[4].
- **Pressured Selling**: Pre-selecting more expensive variations of a product, or pressuring the user to accept the more expensive variations of a product and related products.

SOCIAL PROOF

- **Activity Message:** Informing the user about the activity on the website (e.g. purchases, views or visits).
- **Testimonials:** Testimonials on a product page whose origin is unclear.

SCARCITY

- **Low-Stock Message:** Indicating to users that limited quantities of a product are available, increasing its desirability.
- **High-Demand Message:** Indicating to users that a product is in high demand and likely to sell out soon, increasing its desirability.

OBSTRUCTION

- **Hard to Cancel:** Making it easy for the user to sign up for a service but hard to cancel it.

FORCED ACTION

- **Forced Enrollment:** Coercing users to create accounts or share their information to complete their tasks.

CHAPTER 14
SNEAKING

In the 'reverse pyramid' style of writing, we are taught to be helpful to the reader by starting off with a short summary of what's to come, followed by progressive layers of detail. The idea is that this enables the reader to stop reading at any time and still have an accurate impression of the article. If you want to manipulate the user, you can do the opposite and sneak key information into long paragraphs or poorly labelled sections, so that readers are unlikely to expect it or seek it out. With user interface design, there are many more opportunities to use sneaking, given all the different forms of interaction available: scrolling, progressive disclosure (where the user can click or hover to reveal content on the page), links, buttons, and so forth.[1] In commercial transactions, it can be profitable to hide information, as you can see in the three types of the sneaking deceptive pattern explained below.

THE SNEAK INTO BASKET DECEPTIVE PATTERN

There are several different ways an online retailer could sneak things into a customer's basket. The most brazen approach is to just put it in without mentioning it, and hope the customer either doesn't notice or doesn't care enough to complain. It's also possible to use misdirection and other deceptive patterns to trick users into inadvertently adding items to their basket themselves.

Sneak into basket by Sports Direct: an unwanted £1 magazine

A few years ago, Sports Direct was famous for its giant promotional coffee mugs that everyone in the UK seemed to have in their kitchen cupboards. Let's look at why. Below are screenshots of the *sportsdirect.com* website taken in 2015.

Let's imagine I'm happily browsing the website, about to buy a pair of walking boots. As you can see, there's nothing weird going on. It's just a regular shopping page.[2]

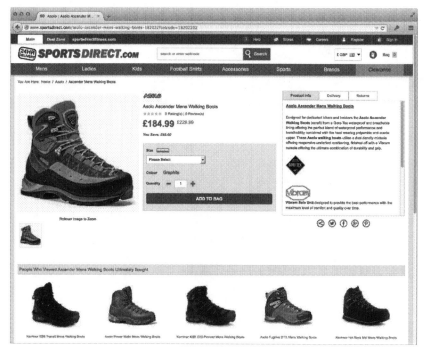

A product detail page on sportsdirect.com in 2015.

Now, let's say I want to buy these boots. I choose my size, click 'add to bag' and then proceed to the checkout.[3] See anything strange?

The checkout page on sportsdirect.com in 2015. An item has been added
without the user's consent.

In a line below the walking boots, there's now an item that I didn't put
into my own shopping basket: a magazine and mug together for £1.
Sports Direct was called out for this on Watchdog, a popular BBC
consumer rights TV show in the UK. In 2014 this practice became
illegal in the EU, thanks to the Consumer Rights Directive.[4]

THE HIDDEN COSTS DECEPTIVE PATTERN

The practice of introducing hidden costs (also known as 'drip pricing'[5]
or 'bait and switch'[6]) involves intentionally introducing a price
increase that the user isn't expecting in the buying journey. More often
than not, this manifests as unexpected fees and charges on the final
checkout page, immediately prior to paying.

Hidden costs by StubHub

An excellent example of hidden costs was published in a research
paper written by researchers Blake et al. in collaboration with StubHub
(the entertainment ticket reseller) in *Marketing Science* journal in April
2021.[7] The paper is well worth reading, since StubHub seemed to be
strangely proud of their own deceptive practices. Be warned though,
the paper does use euphemisms extensively. For example, instead of
talking about hidden costs, it refers to 'back-end fees'.

Here's a visual example of the StubHub user experience. To summarise, the price you see at the beginning of your shopping experience is lower than the price you see at the end; and that's after you've been forced to input your full name, phone number, email and postal address.[8]

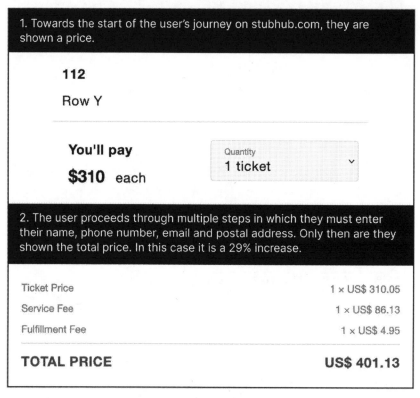

1. Towards the start of the user's journey on stubhub.com, they are shown a price.

112

Row Y

You'll pay

$310 each

Quantity

1 ticket ⌄

2. The user proceeds through multiple steps in which they must enter their name, phone number, email and postal address. Only then are they shown the total price. In this case it is a 29% increase.

Ticket Price	1 × US$ 310.05
Service Fee	1 × US$ 86.13
Fulfillment Fee	1 × US$ 4.95
TOTAL PRICE	**US$ 401.13**

Screenshots of the different prices that StubHub shows for a ticket (1) at the beginning of a user's journey and (2) at the end.

In their research, Blake et al. did an A/B test comparing (A) a design that used hidden costs that were only revealed at the very end (see above) against (B) a design that showed accurate costs at the very start of the user journey. They collected data from several million transactions and it's probably the largest A/B test of deceptive patterns ever published.

Guess what happened. **The users in group A who weren't shown the ticket fees upfront spent about 21% more money and were 14.1% more likely to complete a purchase.** That's huge.

So, now imagine what it would be like to run a business and know that one simple design decision would get your customers to spend 21% more. It's a no brainer – of course you would. One of the only things that would stop you is the threat of legal consequences that would cost more than the profit you'd get from it.

Hidden costs by Airbnb

Resort fees, amenity fees, destination fees and cleaning fees have been common in the hospitality industry for a while. In 2019 Marriott charged cleaning fees of up to 55% of the listed booking price.[9] This behaviour led to them being sued, and the ensuing legal process revealed some staggering internal documents. Marriott knew from its own internal market research that guests were very concerned with the 'lack of transparency' in fees, but they proceeded with it anyway, earning more than $220 million from this practice. An audit also revealed that 33% of the time, resort fees were not shown at the time of booking – the customers only learned about them afterwards! Marriott eventually settled and the company does not engage in this practice any more.[10]

It's not a great case study without any visual examples, so let's move on to Airbnb. For some time now, Airbnb customers have complained on Twitter about additional fees, as you can see below.[11]

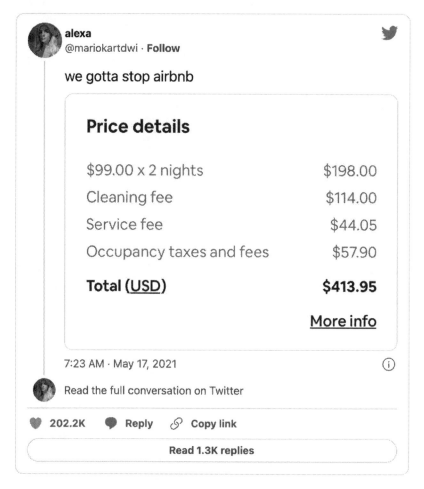

Twitter user alexa complains about Airbnb's additional fees. Her post was popular, with over 200K likes from other Twitter users.

The key question here is whether the fees were hidden at the outset of the user's journey, or whether users like alexa (above) were told in advance but were just unhappy about the high price. The specifics are a little hard to pin down, since Airbnb runs different versions of its user interface in different countries, and it makes regular changes over time. However, these screenshots show what it was like in the United States, around June 2021.[12]

In the screenshot below, you can see a user has selected to travel to Mexico City between 13 and 16 July with two guests. You can see on the map there's a range of different apartments at different prices. Let's imagine that the user selects an apartment at $87/night, since it matches their budget.

Screenshot of airbnb.com search page (US version) from June 2021, courtesy of thepointsguy.com

When the user selects the $87/night apartment, they are taken to the listing details page, shown below. All of a sudden, some additional fees have appeared – a 'Service fee' and 'Occupancy taxes and fees'. This makes the per night cost 35% higher than indicated on the previous page.

$87 / night   ★ **4.88** (193 reviews)

CHECK-IN	CHECKOUT
7/13/2021	7/16/2021

GUESTS
2 guests   ⌄

Reserve

You won't be charged yet

$87 x 3 nights	$261
Service fee	$37
Occupancy taxes and fees	$55
Total	**$353**

Close-up of airbnb.com listing details page (US version) from June 2021, courtesy of thepointsguy.com.

This approach to hidden costs led many users to complain on social media, though notably only in some countries and not others.[13] For example, Airbnb users in Australia do not get tricked with the hidden cost deceptive pattern because their regulator, the Australian Competition and Consumer Commission (ACCC) forbids it.[14] Similarly, Airbnb was pressured by the Norwegian Consumer Authority and the

European Commission in 2019, and it has since given up doing it in Europe.[15] It's interesting to consider how international tech companies vary their use of deceptive patterns by legal jurisdiction. By deduction, the deceptive practices must be profitable enough to continue running in countries where the businesses believe the risk is worth taking, while they turn them off in countries where the regulatory outcome would be too expensive or disruptive. Among other things, this is a very clear sign that regulation works.

If you look at *airbnb.co.uk* today, you'll notice that it has become more transparent with its pricing. When you arrive on the homepage, it defaults to 'any week' in the search area, and the listings are shown on the basis of seven nights, allowing them to calculate the total cost and show it directly as the first price you see.[16]

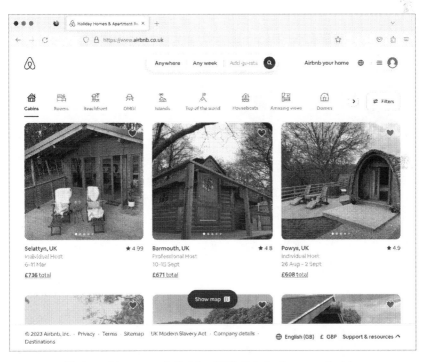

airbnb.co.uk homepage in October 2022. Note the transparent pricing.

Furthermore, if you select your own dates and do a search on *airbnb.co.uk*, you're clearly shown the total price and the per night price. If you click on the total, a small pop-over appears that shows a price breakdown. Bravo, Airbnb. Now do it worldwide.[17]

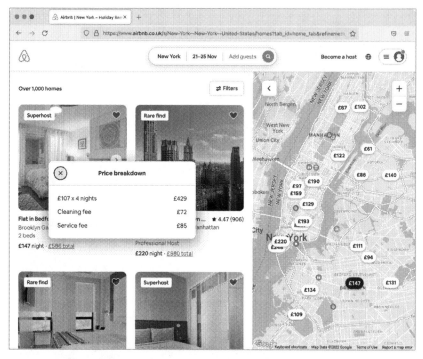

airbnb.co.uk search page with pop-over in October 2022. Note the transparent pricing.

THE HIDDEN SUBSCRIPTION DECEPTIVE PATTERN

Hidden subscription by Figma

If you're a designer, you've probably heard of Figma. It's a collaborative UI design tool used widely in the industry. When you create a design in Figma, you can share it with other people by clicking the helpful blue 'Share' button at the top right of the screen, as shown in the figure below.[18]

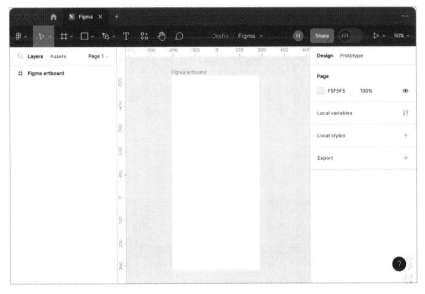

Screenshot of the Figma editor, with a prominent blue 'Share' button at the top right.

Clicking the blue 'Share' button causes a dialog box to appear, which lets you send an invite to another member of your team, or a colleague, or anyone really. From that point, you can then decide if the lucky recipient 'can edit' or 'can view', as shown in this screenshot.[19]

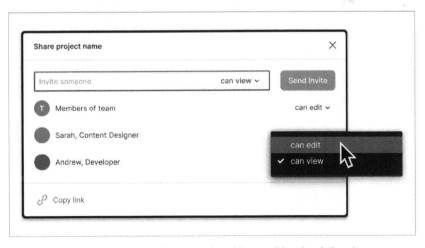

The Figma share dialog, with no mention of the monthly subscription charge that will result from selecting 'can edit' with a new user.

This looks innocent enough. Helpful, you might say. But, as Twitter user Gregor Weichbrodt pointed out in March 2021, if you pick the option 'can edit', then, in the background, this creates a new monthly subscription for the invitee – which you pay for on your credit card. This extra cost is not mentioned in the user interface, anywhere. Since Figma already has your credit card details on file, it'll just start charging you immediately, without any emails or other notifications.[20]

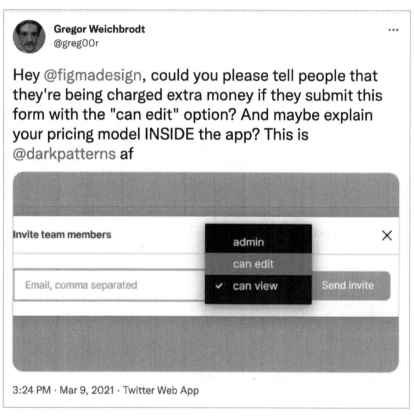

A tweet by Gregor Weichbrodt, angrily complaining about Figma's deceptive pattern.

If you don't pay attention to bills, this sneak into basket deceptive pattern means you end up paying for additional subscriptions that you didn't intend to buy. Think about this for a moment: if you're a large design agency, working with multiple external clients and multiple teams and freelancers, then the risk of being caught out goes up almost exponentially.

Any team member with an editor account can unwittingly create new subscriptions with the 'can edit' option. Those who receive those invitations can then send their own invitations. As most of the design team is unlikely to see the credit card bills or invoices, and the accounts team may have no reason to challenge the costs being incurred by the design team, your business remains ignorant of the fact the monthly subscriptions are going up, every time someone chooses that option.

Hidden subscription by Airtable

It's not clear who copied whom, but *airtable.com* and *figma.com* both use the same deceptive pattern. When users click 'Share' in Airtable, they're taken to a dialog box that's very similar to Figma's (see below). Note that there is no text on this page that explains how clicking 'Send invite' may incur an ongoing subscription fee for each individual added.[21]

Airtable screenshot from the airtable support website.

As you can imagine, this user interface results in some huge unwanted charges, as you can see in this complaint on Twitter by @harper:[22]

just got a $3360 charge from @airtable because i invited some folks to review a base i made. no info that inviting folks would cost $240 a year each.

¯_(ツ)_/¯.

4:20 PM · Jun 15, 2020 · Twitter Web App

Twitter user @harper complains about airtable's deceptive patterns.

If you send the Airtable invite to people with 'editor' or 'creator' selected, then your credit card is automatically – and silently – charged. There's no explanatory text on the page, no warning, no notification. As with Figma, the first time you find out about the extra charges is after you've paid them.

CHAPTER 15
URGENCY

Urgency can be sensible and genuine. There are only so many seats on that flight we want and only so many tickets for that concert, so we know we have to hurry or we'll miss out. This is just the reality of resources in the physical world. But our appreciation of urgency is something that can be abused, and when retailers intentionally create a false sense of urgency, this is a deceptive pattern.

There are two main types of urgency deceptive pattern: fake countdown timers (usually a prominent, animated digital timer shown counting down to zero, whereupon the offer is meant to end – except it doesn't); and fake limited time messages (usually a static piece of content stating that the offer will run out soon).

THE COUNTDOWN TIMER DECEPTIVE PATTERN

Countdown timers on Shopify using the Hurrify merchant app

If you want to start an e-commerce business, Shopify is a great place to start. They make it very easy to set up your store, and they deal with all sorts of complicated things for you, like international tax and shipping. They even have an app store. Surprisingly, the Shopify app store sometimes contains apps that make it easy to create deceptive patterns.

In Shopify's credit, they've been cracking down on this recently, but if you search their app store for terms like 'countdown timer', 'social proof' or 'FOMO' ('fear of missing out'), you'll probably see all sorts of questionable apps in your search results. These sorts of apps can usually be set up in an honest way, but sometimes they enable bad behaviour. For example, up until recently there was a Shopify app called Hurrify, made by a company called Twozillas (It was removed from the Shopify app store some time after I reported it in early 2023). Hurrify was used to create various fake urgency messages, one of which was a fake countdown timer.[1] One of the Twozillas founders, Yousef Khalidi, was interviewed by the Australian Broadcasting Corporation, and was asked about the ethics of the Hurrify app. He replied, 'It's just a tool … it's exactly like a hammer: you can fix stuff with the hammer or you can kill somebody with the hammer.'[2]

Screenshot of Hurrify 'simple text' campaign, taken from the Hurrify app in Shopify.

As you'll see in a moment, Hurrify was by no means as neutrally designed as a hammer, since it was explicitly designed to facilitate deception. You can see an example of Hurrify above, showing what a shopper sees when they view a product page that has been enhanced by a Hurrify campaign: 'Hurry up! Sale ending in 11 Hrs, 59 Mins, 46 Sec. Sale Ends Once The Timer Hits Zero!' An inspection of the Hurrify configuration interface shows that it was designed in a way that enables online businesses to easily show credible-looking but fake countdown timers on their e-commerce product pages. This is shown below:[3]

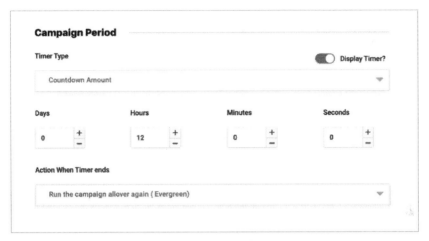

Screenshot of the Hurrify campaign configuration interface.

The bottom dropdown menu is particularly brazen. The dropdown menu 'Action When Timer ends' defaults to 'Run the campaign allover [sic] again (Evergreen)'. This means that the countdown timer is purely cosmetic. It just counts down to zero, goes back to the start and repeats infinitely, serving only to add fake time pressure to the user's shopping experience. In other words, it's a lie.

THE LIMITED TIME MESSAGE DECEPTIVE PATTERN

The limited time message deceptive pattern is very easy to implement since it's just a static piece of text on the page saying that the offer will expire soon – when in reality it won't. Here's an example from samsung.com in which the offer claims 'limited time only'[4], but in actual fact it has been on offer for multiple months (November and December 2022),[5] and the discount was increased by $100 during that period.[6]

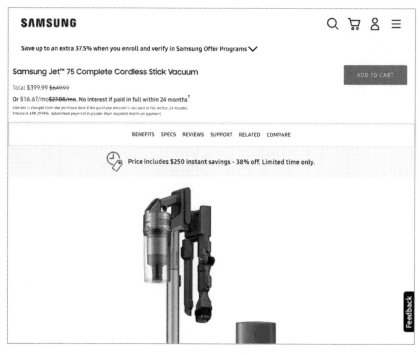

Samsung.com has a 'limited time only' deal that has no end date (December 2022)

CHAPTER 16
MISDIRECTION

Misdirection, like most types of deception, has been practised throughout human history. Whether by a pickpocket, a stage magician, or through the design of a user interface, the principles remain the same:[1]

'Simply stated, misdirection is the psychological technique used to lead or manipulate the spectators' and volunteers' eyes and minds to see what the magician wants them to. Their attention is focused in one direction while the trick is worked elsewhere. Misdirection is not pointing and saying "Look at that!" and then doing something sneaky in the opposite direction. That is a crude form of misdirection that does not work well, nor does it leave a good impression with the audience. The techniques used by good magicians are subtle and sophisticated. So much so that the people in the audience never know they have been manipulated.'

— EDDIE JOSEPH (1992) HOW TO PICK
POCKETS FOR FUN AND PROFIT

THE CONFIRMSHAMING DECEPTIVE PATTERN

The term 'confirmshaming' was popularised by an anonymous blogger who started the confirmshaming tumblr blog in 2016.[2]

Confirmshaming is the use of emotional manipulation to misdirect users, and to push them into opting into something (or opting out of something else).[3] For example, the option to decline may be worded in such a way as to shame you into compliance – you feel so bad about saying no, you end up choosing yes. The most common use of confirmshaming is in mailing list dialogs that pop up when you arrive on a site or via some other trigger.

Confirmshaming by Sears

Here, the retailer Sears uses emotional manipulation and wordplay by labelling the marketing email opt out button, 'No thanks, I hate free money'. This is an archetypal example of confirmshaming. After all, Sears is not offering free money. It is inviting the user to subscribe to a mailing list that will give them a $10 discount on a purchase with Sears.[4]

SEARS

Sign up for our emails and

GET $10 OFF*

example@sears.ca

SIGN ME UP

NO THANKS,
I HATE FREE MONEY

*Offer is valid on online orders of $50 or more, for
new subscribers only. See Privacy Policy. You can
unsubscribe from our emails at any time.

Confirmshaming user interface from Sears in 2017.

Confirmshaming by MyMedic

This example was discovered by Per Axbom. He referred to it as 'the worst example of #confirmshaming I've been subjected to.'[5] MyMedic sells first aid packs and medical supplies. In asking permission for its website to send you notifications, the opt-out link label is presented as 'no, I don't want to stay alive'. This is particularly troubling given that some of its target customers are people likely to be exposed to the trauma of accidents and death in their work.[6]

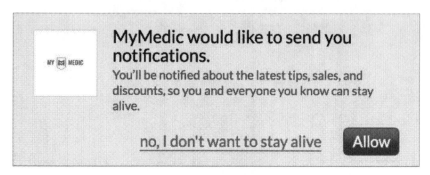

Confirmshaming user interface from MyMedic in August 2021.

THE VISUAL INTERFERENCE DECEPTIVE PATTERN

This deceptive pattern involves hiding content that a user might reasonably expect to be shown on the page. There are several ways to do this.

Visual interference by Trello: pushing users into the expensive 'Business Class' subscription

In January 2021, an anonymous twitter user (@ohhellohellohii) pointed out a deceptive pattern being used by Trello in its sign-up user journey.[7] If you're not familiar with Trello, it's a collaboration tool that lets teams of people view 'cards' of information on a digital board, often used by creative teams. At a glance, a Trello board shows you what's being worked on and who's doing the work.[8]

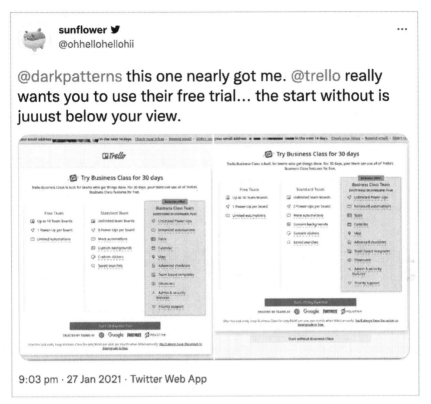

Twitter user @ohhellohellohii complains to Trello about their use of visual interference.

Trello is well known for having a free-to-use plan, which gives people the chance to trial and adopt the platform with a fairly generous allowance of projects and storage space. It's one of the reasons why Trello became popular: people started using it for free, grew to love it, and then upgraded to paid plans. In 2017, Trello was bought by tech giant Atlassian for $425 million. However, in January 2021, the Trello product team used a tweaked sign-up experience that appeared to be an attempt to deliver more fee-paying customers on their most expensive plan, 'Business Class'.

Having clicked an innocent looking 'Sign up' button, users were shown a comparison table with three plans: 'Free Team', 'Standard Team' and 'Business Class Team'. Instead of giving users the means to pick just one, there was a huge green button that said 'Start 30-day free trial'. To all intents and purposes, it appeared there was no other option. However, if users had the presence of mind to scroll down past what seemed to be the bottom of the page, they would find a small grey box labelled 'Start without Business Class' (pictured below).[9]

Close up of Trello screenshot provided by Twitter user @ohhellohellohii.

There were a number of related tricks at work here. Let's take them one by one.

First, there was the issue of hiding a button on the canvas below the bottom of the viewport (aka 'below the fold'). If users' browser windows were too small, they wouldn't see the 'Start without Business Class' button at all. This is about user expectations. They'd have no reason to expect such an important button to be hidden way down there, because users trust businesses to build products in a predictable way.

Trello also used other visual tricks. The boundary of the white box appeared to signify the end of the main content area, and it's a common convention to only place ancillary footer text below this sort of visual divider (like the copyright message and the legalese). In this example, the 'Start without Business Class' button was outside the visual bounds of the main content area, employing visual interference and violating user expectations again.

Finally, we have the difference in visual prominence of the buttons themselves. The 'Start 30-day free trial' button was colourful and high contrast, whereas the 'Start without Business Class' button was muted and low contrast. In fact, it didn't look like a button at all, and it certainly didn't invite users to click it.

At this point, it's also worth saying that if a business takes advantage of visual perception, then it unfairly targets people with visual impairments since they don't have the visual acuity necessary to perceive small or low-contrast text. However, it should be noted that people with serious visual impairments may employ assistive technologies like Apple VoiceOver, a screen reader application that reads pages aloud using a voice synthesiser, and therefore visual deception does not occur.[10]

It's not clear how long Trello kept the offending page live. It may have been an A/B test that was shown to a limited number of people before being discarded. As I write, the sign-up process is now an altogether more honest design:[11]

A more honest upsell page by Trello, where the option to opt out of the premium trial ('Skip') is shown relatively prominently.

Visual interference by YouTube: a near-invisible close button

'Freemium' is a portmanteau, a word that smashes two terms together to create a new, if somewhat clumsy term. If a service is freemium – a combination of 'free' and 'premium' – then it's offering a two-tier pricing strategy to consumers. One approach to freemium involves letting users have a free account indefinitely with no contract, but then to persuade those users to upgrade and pay for a premium account that has extra features. It's become a commonplace online commercial strategy, because – well, who doesn't want something for free? By having a huge free user-base, the business gets an audience on whom they can test various persuasive tactics.

In January 2021, Twitter user @bigslabomeat pointed out that YouTube was deploying a deceptive pattern that would get users to sign up for a premium free trial.[12] As you'll see, users weren't given an obvious means to continue with the free tier product. Rather, they needed to take notice of a tiny, low contrast X at the top right of the page, and deduce that tapping the X would then effectively reject the offer of the free trial. A classic example of visual interference.[13]

⟲ **Dark Patterns** Retweeted

Bigolslabomeat
@bigolslabomeat   ...

Getting desperate now? This came up when I opened
the @YouTube app. I don't want premium. I don't want
a trial. I've said that at least a hundred times so far,
now this without even a close button. Talk about
@darkpatterns

▶ YouTube Premium

Don't miss the perks of Premium

Try YouTube Premium. We'll email you seven days
before your trial ends.

1 MONTH FREE

9:11 am · 20 Jan 2021 · Twitter for Android

Screenshot of YouTube employing visual interference. The close button X is
visually obscured by the model's hair.

Visual interference by Tesla: non-refundable accidental app purchases

At the end of 2019, Tesla introduced a new feature to its mobile app. Put simply, the updated app let Tesla car owners buy upgrades for their vehicles, such as an autopilot that would unlock 'Full Self-Driving' capabilities.[14] At over $4,000, these were significant add-ons.

After this feature was introduced, a number of Tesla car owners made it known that they'd made a new feature purchase by mistake, and Tesla was refusing to provide any refunds. Journalist Ted Stein provided an analysis, describing the nature of the techniques used.[15] On the payment screen, the wording 'Upgrades cannot be refunded' appeared in small, very low contrast dark grey text on a black background, effectively hiding it from users.[16]

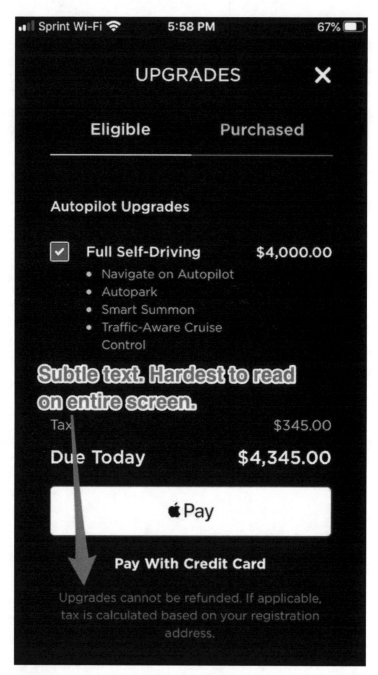

Tesla's mobile app refusing refunds on accidental purchases (Stein, 2020).

Tesla customer (and well-known author) Nassim Nicholas Taleb ran into this problem in January 2020 and he asked for a refund. He received a denial from Tesla's customer support, which he published on Twitter.[17] They told him 'there are not refunds available for software purchases. This would be similar to the situation of paying for an addition to a house, deciding you don't like it, and then requesting a refund from the contractor.' Taleb replied:

'The purchase was non-intentional. I unintentionally hit the buy button while the app was in my pocket and do not know of any app that makes you do a purchase of $4,333 without confirmation/password or something of the sort. [...] Even Amazon makes it hard to buy a $6.99 Kindle books has reversed purchases made in error [...] I did not TRY your software, and I DID NOT USE your stupid software [...] You have a flawed app.'

If everything that Taleb asserts in his email is true, then as well as visual interference (shown in the figure above), Tesla also appears to have used the 'obstruction' deceptive pattern, making it hard to cancel.

At some point after this complaint was made, Tesla reversed its position and added a 48-hour cancellation window for this type of in-app purchase. This is shown in the figure below, though you may need a magnifying glass to see it, as it is written in dark grey text on a black background.[18]

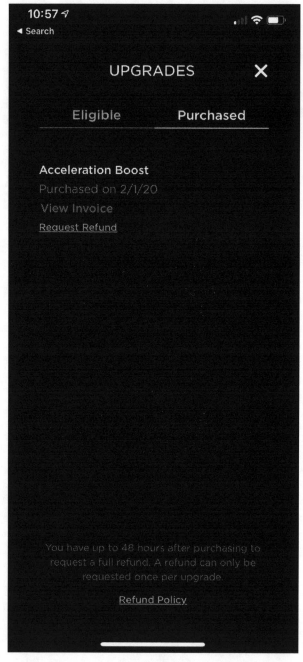

Tesla's refund policy, which appeared after Taleb's complaint.

THE TRICK WORDING DECEPTIVE PATTERN

The trick wording deceptive pattern is employed to confuse or mislead users into taking actions that they would not have taken had they fully understood the situation at the time. This manipulation is achieved through ambiguous phrasing, double negatives, or strategically placed information within sentences or user interfaces.

Trick wording by the Trump presidential campaign

In this example, the Trump campaign used a variety of different deceptive patterns, trick wording being just one of them. In March 2021, I was contacted by Shane Goldmacher, a reporter from the New York Times. He'd found some examples of serious deceptive patterns in the Trump campaign donation portal and he wanted to talk through his findings before going public with his conclusions. Goldmacher's article provides a detailed account of his findings, and I'll summarise it here.[19] Users were typically driven to the donation portal via email campaigns. Over time, the Trump campaign dialled up the severity of deceptive patterns. They started by using a preselected checkbox that turned a one-off donation into a recurring donation, as shown below:[20]

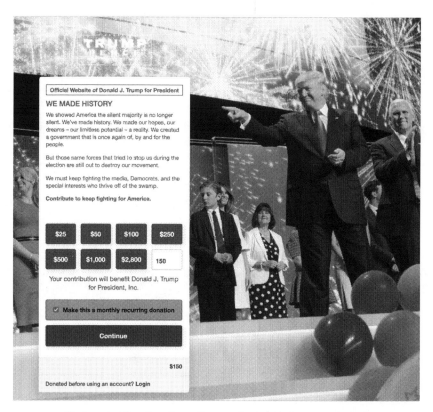

Trump campaign deceptive pattern version 1, featuring a preselected checkbox for 'Make this a monthly recurring donation' (in this case the user has entered $150 as their chosen donation amount).

This approach makes use of the default effect cognitive bias, which can be considered a variation of the sneaking deceptive pattern. There are lots of reasons why this is a powerful tool. First, there's simply the matter of awareness – users have to notice the box, then they have to read what's in the box, and then they have to work out what it all means. If the user doesn't invest time and effort in those interactions, they'll scroll past the preselected checkbox completely unaware of the implications.

There are other, more subtle psychological effects. For example, the preselected checkbox may cause some people to feel social pressure. In other words, they may feel that other people like them would leave the box ticked, so they should too (the social proof cognitive bias).

In any case, the Trump campaign discovered that these preselected checkboxes worked well, so a few weeks later they decided to add another preselected checkbox next to it. In Goldmacher's investigation he discovered that they called this the 'money bomb', which shows that they knew the implications of what they were doing. Version 2 is shown below. The first preselected checkbox worked the same way as in version 1, creating a recurring payment every month. The second preselected checkbox served to take an additional sum of money – the same amount again, for 'Trump's birthday'.

Trump campaign deceptive pattern version 2, with two preselected checkboxes.

This design was so effective that they decided to dial up the severity even more. In the example above, you can see the top checkbox sets up a monthly donation. They decided to make this weekly, as you can see below. And the second checkbox was updated to indicate a donation of $100 extra (even if the user's chosen recurring donation value was much lower than that).

☑ **Join the President's Executive Club - For true patriots only**
Make this a weekly recurring donation until 11/3

☑ **President Trump: CONGRATS!! YOU'VE been selected as our End-of-Quarter MVP! Join the Cash Blitz NOW and make it official**
Donate an additional $100 automatically on 9/30

Trump campaign deceptive pattern version 3, using two preselected checkboxes.

Believe it or not, they took it to yet another level in version 4 of this design. They introduced trick wording and visual interference to make the purpose of these preselected checkboxes less obvious. As you can see below, the bold text doesn't refer to the charges at all; that information is shown below in a thinner, less obvious font that might easily be skipped over by the reader.

☑ **This is the FINAL month until Election Day and we need EVERY Patriot stepping up if we're going to WIN FOUR MORE YEARS for President Trump. He's revitalizing our economy, restoring LAW & ORDER, and returning us to American Greatness, but he's not done yet. This is your chance - stand with President Trump & MAXIMIZE your impact NOW!**
Make this a weekly recurring donation until 11/3

☑ **President Trump: October 9th marks 25 days out from Election Day and we need your support. American Patriots like YOU inspired me to keep fighting this past week, and I'm not done yet. I'm asking you to join Operation MAGA and help me secure VICTORY in November. Join the movement NOW**
Donate an additional $100 automatically on 10/09

Trump campaign deceptive pattern version 4, featuring two preselected checkboxes with severe visual interference.

One of the most remarkable aspects of Goldmacher's investigation was his discovery of the timeline involved. He proved the points at which these deceptive activities were introduced, and was able to show the data against the refund rates demanded from Trump campaign subscribers compared with subscribers to the Biden campaign. Overall, the Trump campaign had to give $122 million in refunds while the Biden campaign only gave $21 million.

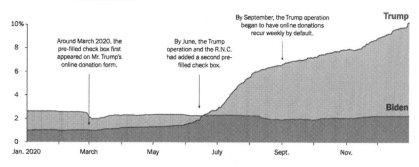

How Refunds to Trump Donors Soared in 2020
Refunds are shown as the percentage of money received by each operation to date via WinRed and ActBlue.

Chart by Eleanor Lutz and Rachel Shorey from the New York Times article 'How Trump Steered Supporters Into Unwitting Donations'.

It's safe to say that only a small proportion of people who'd been caught out by these deceptive patterns would have gone through the process of realising, deciding to take action, investing the time to take action, and successfully getting a refund. The rest would have simply been charged, suffered a financial loss, and carried on with their lives. Goldmacher interviewed one donor, a 78-year-old Californian, Victor Amelino, who'd made an online donation for $990 that recurred seven more times before he realised. In total, he contributed almost $8,000 to the Trump campaign. 'Bandits!' he said. 'I'm retired. I can't afford to pay all that damn money.'

Ryanair's use of the trick wording deceptive pattern

Ryanair used a combination of deceptive patterns that included trick wording for a few years, from roughly 2010 to 2013. The screenshot below sums it up perfectly.[21] Here, the airline Ryanair makes it look like travel insurance is mandatory when you're buying a flight. However, there's a hidden way of opting out. In the dropdown box labelled 'Please select a country of residence', the user can find the option, 'Don't insure me' listed between the two countries Denmark and Finland. Many users won't expect this highly unusual approach to opting out, and may end up buying insurance unaware they had a choice not to. Arguably this could be described as using the visual interference deceptive pattern as well as trick wording, since the page layout and form field style contribute to the nature of the misdirection.

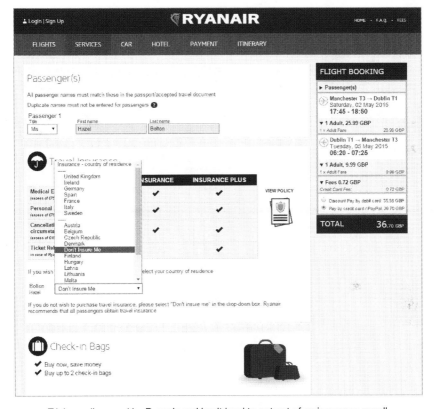

Trick wording used by Ryanair, making it hard to opt out of an insurance upsell.

In 2015, this deceptive pattern led to Ryanair being fined €850,000 by the Italian competition authority (ACGM).[22] Despite this fine, Ryanair have continued to use various deceptive patterns, leading the Norwegian Consumer Council to send them a letter in 2022, asking them to stop.[23]

PRESSURED SELLING

Pressured selling involves putting pressure on users to complete a purchase by employing a combination of deceptive tricks and cognitive biases, including scarcity and anchoring.

Pressured selling by Booking.com

Pressured selling and other deceptive patterns were used so extensively by hotel booking platforms in the 2010s that the entire industry ended up being scrutinised by regulators in a number of different jurisdictions. For example, in 2017 the UK's Competition and Markets Authority (CMA) carried out an investigation into Booking.com, Hotels.com, Expedia, ebookers.com, Agoda and Trivago, among others.[24] The outcome of this was a new set of strict guidelines to ensure that they stayed on the right side of the existing legislation.[25] This is interesting because it shows how there can be a bit of a gap between laws and how they get interpreted by businesses. These new guidelines were effectively intended to plug that gap and make it very clear what is and what isn't allowed.

Let's take a look at Booking.com in 2017 to see the kinds of pressured selling techniques it was using at the time. The screenshot below is from an article by software developer Roman Cheplyaka titled 'How Booking.com manipulates you':[26]

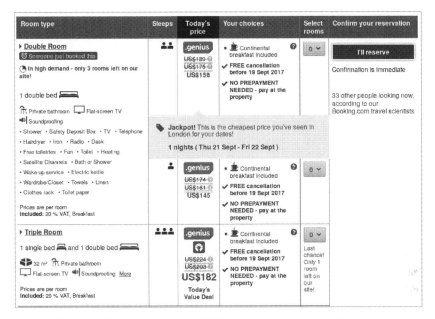

Screenshot from Booking.com in 2017, featuring various forms of pressure selling.

This is what you would have seen on a Booking.com hotel page in 2017. Starting from the top left, it says in the red box with a small alarm clock icon, 'Someone just booked this'. According to Cheplyaka, this is animated: 'it pops up one or two seconds later, making it seem like a realtime notification – an impression reinforced by the alarm clock icon. To be clear, it is not realtime, and there is no reason to delay its display other than to trick you'. Cheplyaka subsequently found that if he hovered his cursor over the sentence long enough, it revealed another sentence, in this case 'Last booked: 4 hours ago'. So, the word 'just' and the timed appearance was really stretching the truth.

Also, if we look at the rest of the sentence more closely, what does it really mean? 'Someone just booked this'. Does it mean someone just booked this room within your date range, thereby reducing the availability of similar rooms for you? Or did they book it on completely different dates, thereby making the warning completely irrelevant? We don't know for sure, but after their investigation, the CMA announced that Booking.com and others agreed to:

'not giving a false impression of the availability or popularity of a hotel or rushing customers into making a booking decision based on incomplete information. **For example, when highlighting that other customers are looking at the same hotel as you, making it clear they may be searching for different dates**' (emphasis added)[27]

We can't be sure, but it sounds like the hotel booking sites the CMA investigated were caught red-handed doing this – after all, why else would this new rule have been created? There are a few other statements in this screenshot that could be using the same trick: 'In high demand – only 3 rooms left on our site!'; '33 other people looking now, according to our Booking.com travel scientists'; and 'Last chance! Only 1 room left on our site!'

Let's move on. If you gaze across to the right, you'll see a box with the text 'Jackpot! This is the cheapest price you've seen in London for your dates!' Cheplyaka points out that this statement is tautological. It's the first price the user has been shown, so it's probably being considered a sample of one item. By being the only item you've seen in London for your dates, it is the cheapest. It's also the most expensive.

Now let's look at the struck out prices. For all the rooms, it looks like they've been discounted twice. For example, the top room started at $189, then down to $175, and now it's at $158. But Cheplyaka found that if he hovered his cursor over the price long enough, this appeared:

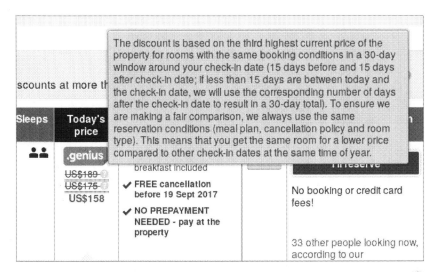

The discount is based on the third highest current price of the property for rooms with the same booking conditions in a 30-day window around your check-in date (15 days before and 15 days after check-in date; if less than 15 days are between today and the check-in date, we will use the corresponding number of days after the check-in date to result in a 30-day total). To ensure we are making a fair comparison, we always use the same reservation conditions (meal plan, cancellation policy and room type). This means that you get the same room for a lower price compared to other check-in dates at the same time of year.

scounts at more th

Sleeps	Today's price	.genius
👤👤	US$189 US$175 US$158	breakfast included ✔ FREE cancellation before 19 Sept 2017 ✔ NO PREPAYMENT NEEDED - pay at the property

Reserve

No booking or credit card fees!

33 other people looking now, according to our

A screenshot of Booking.com from 2017 in which key information is hidden and is only revealed when the user happens to hover their cursor over a small text link.

It's very wordy and you'd be forgiven for not reading the whole thing, not least because if you move your mouse by a fraction, it'll disappear. It explains that the statement is once again not based on your specific dates! It's based on a month-long window around your dates. So if you didn't see this pop-up, you'd be none the wiser and think you're eligible for a special discount on your dates when, in fact, you're not.

As well as pressured selling, the deceptive patterns we've looked at here can also be described as trick wording (described in the previous section). Deceptive patterns often overlap like this. It's reminiscent of evil gods and genies from folk stories that use wordplay and pedantry to inflict horrible consequences on those who beg wishes from them. When the Greek goddess Eos asked Zeus to give her lover Tithonus immortality, he granted her wish, noting that she forgot to ask for eternal youth. Tithonus lived forever, but became so old and wrinkled that Eos eventually abandoned him. The lesson here is that if you want immortality, don't ask Zeus – or any popular hotel booking websites for that matter.

CHAPTER 17
SOCIAL PROOF

This category of deceptive pattern involves taking advantage of the social proof cognitive bias, in which people tend to follow the actions of others in order to determine their own behaviour. There are two main types of social proof deceptive patterns: the activity message deceptive pattern, and the testimonial deceptive pattern.

THE ACTIVITY MESSAGE DECEPTIVE PATTERN

We've all seen an activity message before. It's a little notification that appears on an e-commerce store that tries to persuade you to make a purchase by showing you some sort of message about social activity. Of course, if the message is true then it's a perfectly acceptable practice. It can be quite useful to know what products are popular in a store – it's similar to seeing a queue on a street outside a shop, or seeing lots of shoppers holding the same item when queuing to check out. It's a feature you get for free in the real world, but it's very easy to fake online. The example below was shared by Henry Neves-Charge on Twitter in 2017.[1]

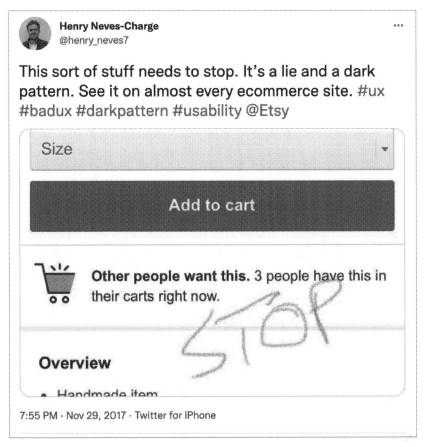

Henry Neves-Charge
@henry_neves7   •••

This sort of stuff needs to stop. It's a lie and a dark
pattern. See it on almost every ecommerce site. #ux
#badux #darkpattern #usability @Etsy

Size ▾

Add to cart

Other people want this. 3 people have this in
their carts right now.

Overview

• Handmade item

7:55 PM · Nov 29, 2017 · Twitter for iPhone

Twitter user Henry Neves-Charge alleges that Esty uses the activity message
deceptive pattern.

Fake activity with Beeketing's Sales Pop app

If you don't have the time or the skills to build your own deceptive
patterns, you can actually buy plug-ins for your website that let you
add deceptive patterns very easily. As I explained earlier, the Shopify
app store sometimes contains a few of them. These apps manage to
sneak in by offering tools that can be either used legitimately or configured to deceive users. Other e-commerce platforms have the same sort
of problem, including BigCommerce, Weebly and WooCommerce.

In 2019, Shopify removed fourteen apps from its app store, many of which could be configured to deliver deceptive patterns with just a few clicks.[2] Twelve of them were provided by a company called Beeketing. Here's one of the Beeketing apps: Sales Pop. It causes an activity message overlay to appear on screen containing claims like '9 customers have bought item x together with item y' or 'Alycia in San Francisco just bought item x 4 minutes ago'.[3]

Stylised depiction of the Sales Pop app, from the Beeketing website.

What's surprising is that Beeketing actively encourages store owners to set this up deceptively. In the Sales Pop app's support documentation, Beeketing give a barefaced confession[4]:

'This guide is applied for all the supported platforms except for Shopify. The reason behind it is the recent changes in Shopify policies. There will be no custom notification anymore. Custom notification used to be a highly effective way to create urgency and scarcity for your store. Nevertheless, since the Shopify's requirement to use real data instead of made-up one, custom notification was left out.'

– BEEKETING (2019)

Here's how easy it is to create a deceptive custom notification using Beeketing Sales Pop. At the time of writing, this is still available for BigCommerce, Weebly and WooCommerce.[5]

Location

○ Random locations

◉ Manually select locations

> Eg: San Francisco, United States
> New York, United States

Customer location (separated by new line)

☐ Popup show at specific pages

☒ Custom notifications will have random 'time ago' within 12 hours after they are created

❗ There will be 0 new notification(s) created

Create now

Close-up of the Sales Pop custom notification configuration page from the Beeketing website.

As you can see in the screenshot, the merchant picks the locations they want announced in the activity message – either random or manually selected (after all, if they run a local bakery it would look suspicious if the notification showed an order from 3,000 miles away. No sensible human would order perishable goods from such a distance, so the manual option lets them put in a list of local-sounding places). Then, the merchant can tick a checkbox to have the notifications receive a random 'time ago' label up within a 12 hour window, making them look more realistic.

THE TESTIMONIAL DECEPTIVE PATTERN

The testimonial deceptive pattern is an easy one for unscrupulous companies to employ, since it just involves writing something positive about your offering, and then attributing it to a customer. Like this: 'Harry Brignull's book on deceptive design may be the best book ever written. —Abraham Lincoln, 1861.'

Now, I know what you're thinking. This is just false advertising. It's been around for decades and it's already regulated. This is indeed true. But even though it's well known, it's still common. What's more, it's often used in tandem with other deceptive patterns to create a web of pressure and deception. For this reason, it's worthy of being listed together with the other deceptive patterns. For example, a recent FTC staff report[6] describes a civil suit that it pursued against RagingBull resulting in a $2.4 million settlement.[7] It is notable that it describes the deceptive practices as working together to create a 'compounding effect':

'In *Raging Bull*, for instance, the FTC alleged that the operators of an online stock trading site used **deceptive customer testimonials to lure consumers in**, hid purported disclaimers in dense terms and conditions text boxes that required scrolling to find, and sold services as a subscription but made it difficult to cancel and stop the recurring charges. **The combination of these dark patterns**

had a compounding effect, increasing the impact of each and exacerbating the harm to the consumer.' (emphasis added)

— FTC STAFF REPORT (2022)

CHAPTER 18
SCARCITY

The scarcity category of deceptive pattern involves falsely claiming that a product or service is in limited supply, encouraging customers to quickly complete a purchase before the stock runs out. The scarcity deceptive pattern is similar to the urgency deceptive pattern, but urgency is time-based, while scarcity is materials-based.

THE LOW STOCK MESSAGE DECEPTIVE PATTERN

HeyMerch's Shopify app Hey!Scarcity Low Stock Counter is a great example of the low stock message deceptive pattern. This app makes it easy for shop owners to show fake low stock messages like this (outlined below).[1]

The low stock message generated by the HeyMerch Hey!Scarcity Low Stock Counter app (2022).

HeyMerch doesn't try to hide their intentions, either. Their admin interface encourages merchants to use randomly generated fake figures, as you can see below: 'Generate the stock data between [3] and [5]'. By the time you read this, it's possible it may have been banned by Shopify, since their rules explicitly forbid 'apps that falsify data to deceive merchants or buyers.'[2]

Data

○ Use the real stock data

☐ Show the available stock data if it is less than   6 ⌃⌄

● Generate stock data between   3 ⌃⌄   and   5 ⌃⌄

Close-up of the admin interface, clearly showing the ability to generate fake low stock messages (2022)

THE HIGH DEMAND MESSAGE DECEPTIVE PATTERN

The high demand message deceptive pattern is the lazy version of the low stock message. It is simply some text on the page that falsely claims that the item is in high demand. The Scarcity++ Low Stock Counter app by Effective Apps enhances this by adding an animation to the high-demand message, thus drawing attention to it.[3] As you can see in the screenshot below, the creators recommend using the message 'Low in stock!' and they suggest configuring the app when the stock level drops below 'a large number (like 1000000) if you'd like the alert to appear for all of your products'.[4]

I'm sure you'll agree that a stock level in the hundreds of thousands cannot be described as 'low stock' – it's a lie. Perhaps by the time you read this, this product will have been improved or removed from the Shopify app store.

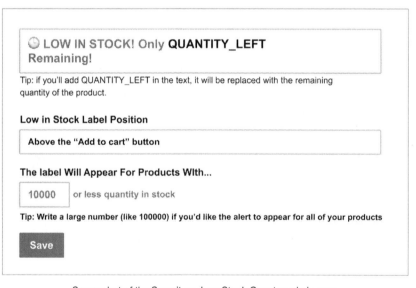

Screenshot of the Scarcity++ Low Stock Counter admin area.

CHAPTER 19
OBSTRUCTION

In part 2, I explained how purposefully difficult-to-use UI design (sludge) can be employed as part of an exploitative resource depletion strategy, to make users fatigued and give up trying to achieve their goals, or to soften them up prior to a bigger deception. This is exactly what the obstruction category of deceptive pattern is all about.

Obstruction in Facebook and Google's privacy settings

When the GDPR came into effect in the EU, companies were obliged to change the way they presented their privacy options to ensure that users had the means to consent (or dissent) to proposed uses of their personal data. This consent needed to be 'freely given, specific, informed and unambiguous' (article 4(11)).[1]

On behalf of its citizens, in 2018 the publicly funded Norwegian Consumer Council (Forbrukerrådet) carried out an investigation into this practice.[2] It found that Facebook and Google had used deceptive patterns in their user interfaces to 'nudge users away from the privacy-friendly choices'. They did this by using obstruction: they made it easy to accept the privacy-invading settings and hard to reject them. You can see this in the figure below. It's one click to 'accept and continue', but if the user wants to 'reject and continue', there is no equivalent button. Instead, they have to click the ambiguously labelled 'manage data settings' button, and then they have to push an ambiguous toggle to the left. Notice that the toggle is improperly labelled – the user is not clearly told whether they have successfully rejected the ad tracking.[3]

Facebook's data settings (Forbrukerrådet, 2018).

Google's approach was similar. Google required users to sign in first, and to then look for and use the privacy settings dashboard of their own volition. From there, the user could choose to opt out. Again, this is obstruction, and it is the opposite of what the GDPR regulation requires.[4]

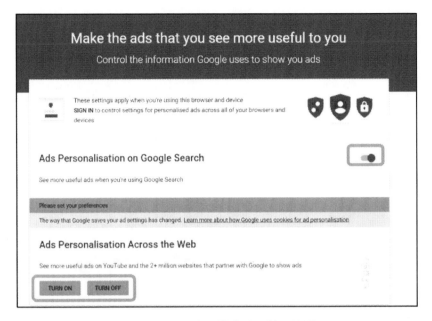

Google's data settings (Forbrukerrådet, 2018).

In both examples, users were required to expend more effort and attention to opt out than to just go along with the defaults and be automatically opted in. The Norwegian Consumer Council argued this was an example of the default effect bias being employed as a deceptive pattern for commercial gain.

In 2018, the Norwegian Consumer Council filed a complaint against Google on this matter. Five years later, they are still waiting for a final decision by the Irish Data Protection Commissioner.

In 2022, ten European consumer groups filed a second complaint against Google for employing similar tactics but with a greater focus on location data and the Google account sign up process.[5] As BEUC writes: 'Tech giant Google is unfairly steering consumers towards its surveillance system when they sign up to a Google account, instead of giving them privacy by design and by default as required by the General Data Protection Regulation (GDPR).'

THE HARD TO CANCEL DECEPTIVE PATTERN

Hard to cancel is a type of obstruction that involves businesses making it difficult for users to cancel their subscriptions. It is often paired up with a very easy and frictionless subscription experience – making it easy to join and hard to leave. When seen in this pairing, it is sometimes referred to as a 'roach motel' – a humorous reference to a pest control device of the same name.[6]

Hard to cancel by the New York Times

The New York Times has published a number of articles on deceptive patterns over the years, and it holds a progressive view on consumer rights and regulation. However, until recently, it did not extend that view to its own digital services, and it is famous for using the hard to cancel deceptive pattern.

As Twitter user @vanillatary succinctly put it: 'this should literally be illegal […] the extra subscriptions they keep by making it annoying and time consuming to unsubscribe are clearly worth far more than the cost of hiring additional staff to handle the unsubscribe calls, which could've been handled 100 times more efficiently by a few lines of web code […] So some % of the NYT's business model is based on holding on to paid customers who no longer actually consider their product worth the cost'.[7]

The screenshots below show an easy-to-follow subscription process on the one hand, and an obstructive cancellation process on the other. Instead of giving the user a button to directly cancel a subscription, the NYT provided instructions on contacting customer services.[8]

The New York Times

SPECIAL OFFER

Unlimited access to all the journalism we offer.

~~€2~~ €0.50/week

Billed as ~~€8~~ €2 every 4 weeks for one year.

SUBSCRIBE NOW

Cancel or pause anytime.

A typical New York Times subscription upsell page in November 2021, provided by Twitter user @vanillatary.

Cancel your subscription

There are several ways to unsubscribe from The Times. Once your subscription has been cancelled you will have limited access to The New York Times's content.

Speak with a Customer Care Advocate

Call us at 866-273-3612 if you are in the U.S. Our hours are 7 a.m. to 10 p.m. E.T. Monday to Friday, and 7 a.m. to 3 p.m. E.T. on weekends and holidays.

Please see our international contact information if you are outside of the U.S.

Chat with a Customer Care Advocate

Click the "Chat" button to the right or bottom of this page to chat with a Care Advocate. Chat is accessible 24 hours a day 7 days a week.

For more information about our cancellation policy, see our Terms of Sale.

The New York Times subscription cancellation page, provided by Twitter user @vanillatary in November 2021.

In February 2021, someone published a transcript of their NYT live chat cancellation experience, which showed the process had taken 17 minutes, start to finish.[9] I tried it too, here in the UK, on 13 November 2021. It took me 7 minutes to cancel my subscription. The chat representative asked me why I was cancelling, and then used my reason as a hook to start what I presume was a scripted attempt to change my mind.

You may be wondering if 7 minutes is really that long. Well, if we compare it to the approximately 500 milliseconds it would have taken to submit the same request via a button on a web page, it's over 800 times longer. That's a big difference.

In September 2021, the New York Times fell foul of a class action lawsuit on issues relating to its automatic renewal experience. Mainly, its transgressions fell under California's Automatic Renewal Law, which states among other things:[10]

> 'a business that allows a consumer to accept an automatic renewal or continuous service offer online shall allow a consumer to terminate the automatic renewal or continuous service exclusively online, at will, and without engaging any further steps that obstruct or delay the consumer's ability to terminate the automatic renewal or continuous service immediately.'

This suit mandated the payment of over $5 million in settlement fees.[11] For a period, the newspaper added the means to cancel online for California residents, then in early 2023 it extended this for all customers, regardless of their location. In a similar class action lawsuit, the Washington Post was found to be deploying similar deceptive patterns, making it difficult for users to cancel subscriptions.[12] It too had to pay a settlement, this time for $6.8 million. The FTC also brought a similar complaint against online education provider ABCmouse, in which 'ABCmouse didn't clearly tell parents that their subscriptions would renew automatically, and then the company made it very difficult for them to cancel'.[13] The company had to pay $10 million in damages, and – thankfully – was also told to stop employing these deceptive patterns.

Hard to cancel by Amazon Prime

In 2021, sixteen consumer organisations in the EU and the US filed complaints against Amazon for employing the hard to cancel deceptive pattern against users who wished to cancel their Amazon Prime subscriptions. In a report titled 'You can log out but you can never leave', the Norwegian Consumer Council explained the process of cancellation, which involved a labyrinth of confusing choices, shown below.[14]

Steps 1-6 in cancelling an Amazon Prime subscription (Norwegian Consumer Council, 2021).

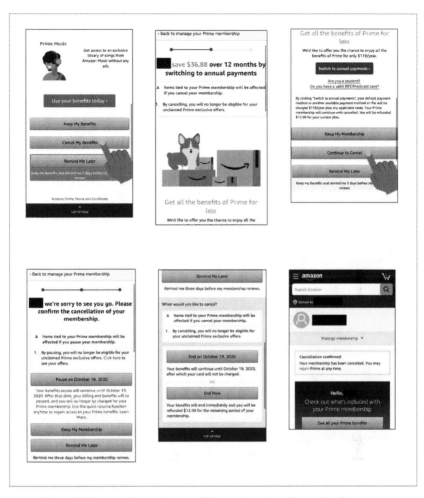

Steps 7-12 in cancelling an Amazon Prime subscription (Norwegian Consumer
Council, 2021).

In response to the slew of complaints, the European Commission ran
an investigation that they concluded by instructing Amazon to change
the cancellation procedure for all European consumers.[15] The
European Commissioner gave a strongly worded statement, saying:

'Opting for an online subscription can be very handy for
consumers as it is often a very straightforward process, but the

reverse action of unsubscribing should be just as easy. Consumers must be able to exercise their rights without any pressure from platforms. One thing is clear: manipulative design or "dark patterns" must be banned.'

At roughly the same time, seven US consumer groups wrote a letter to the FTC, asking them to investigate – and it did.[16] During the investigation, internal documents were leaked to the business news site Insider.com, who revealed that Amazon had knowingly implemented deceptive patterns as a part of a strategy to retain customers and reduce churn.[17] Leaked documents admitted things like: 'The button's label "Continue with FREE 1-day shipping" did not adequately convey that the customer was signing up for a membership'; 'Unintentional sign-ups erode customer trust'; and 'Either way, improvements in clarity during sign-up are needed'. Furthermore, data leaked in August 2017 also showed that 67% of the cancellation requests directly handled by the Prime team were related to 'accidental sign-ups'. In other words, the evidence implies that Amazon knew exactly what it was doing and continued anyway.

The FTC's Amazon investigation still seems to be ongoing at the time of writing. In March 2023, the FTC proposed some new rules on the hard to cancel deceptive pattern. 'The proposed rule would require that companies make it as easy to cancel a subscription as it is to sign up for one' said FTC Chair Lina M Khan.[18] This was even supported by President Biden, who tweeted: 'I support @FTC's proposal requiring companies to fix this. It shouldn't be harder to cancel a service than it was to subscribe for it'.[19]

Amazingly, even after all this, cancelling an Amazon Prime subscription is still not as easy as it could be. The fact that Amazon is willing to spend so much money in legal proceedings and take on this much risk gives us a clue as to how profitable this practice must be.

CHAPTER 20
FORCED ACTION

Forced action is a category of deceptive pattern in which a business offers users something they want – but forces them to do something in return. This is a problem when the forced action runs contrary to a reasonable user's expectations, or when it contradicts laws or regulations.

One of the most well-known and amusingly named types of forced action is 'privacy zuckering', named, of course, after Mark Zuckerberg.[1] The user is tantalised by a service or product and in the process of trying to get it, they are tricked into sharing personal data with the business, and also tricked into giving the business permission to use that data for profit-making endeavours – like selling it, sharing it or using it for targeted advertising.

The issue here isn't that data sharing, data sales or targeted advertising are necessarily bad – because they are legitimate business models when done correctly. The issue is the lack of the user's *consent* for this to happen. It doesn't count as consent if the user has been tricked or coerced. Consent must be 'freely given, specific, informed and unambiguous' – the exact language used, in fact, in the EU's GDPR.

Here's an example of forced action, observed by security researcher Brian Krebs.[2] When a user installs Skype on their iPad, they are taken through a series of log-in steps. One of the steps requires the user to upload their personal address book from their iPad to Skype (a division of Microsoft). There is no option to decline (shown below), and the page does not explain that the next step (the iOS permissions dialog) will actually give them the choice to decline, and that declining will not have an effect on their ability to use Skype.[3]

Screenshot of the forced action deceptive pattern in the Skype iPad app (2022).

If we look at a subsequent step (below), we can see that the designers certainly know how to design a clear opt-out when they want to.[4] The options 'Yes, contribute' and 'No, do not contribute' are equally weighted, obvious and easy to understand. This further highlights the forced action and coercive wording on the 'Find Contacts Easily' step (above).

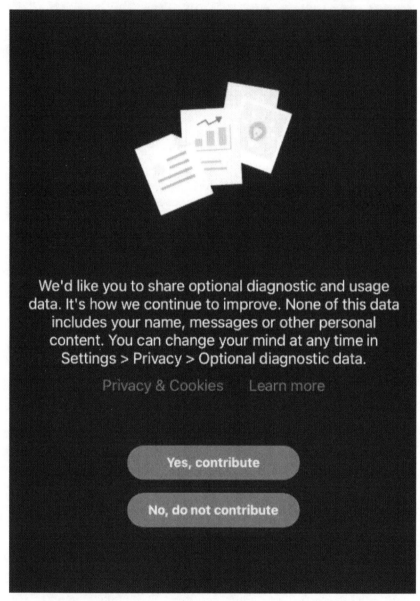

Screenshot of a different Skype iPad app dialog, in which the means to opt out is easy (2022).

So why is contact sharing something that users may want to opt out of? This is essentially a question about the right to privacy. The book *Privacy's Blueprint* by Woodrow Hartzog (2018) covers this,[5] including an analysis of the overlap between deceptive patterns and privacy, which Hartzog refers to as 'the problem of extracted consent', also known as 'consent washing' (Wylie, 2019).[6]

One of the issues is that it's not just about the privacy of the user – it's about the privacy of the people in their address book too. The contacts themselves may not want to give their permission. Their existence in the address book may be confidential (perhaps the user is a journalist or a lawyer), their labelling in the address book may be confidential ('Alex, my secret lover'), and the graph data (that is, the connection between the address book holder and other contacts) may be confidential too. Finally, there is also the matter of what Microsoft intends to do with the data once it is uploaded. The page says 'Find Contacts Easily', which sounds pleasant enough, but there's also a ton of information in the 'Privacy & Cookies' and 'Learn more' pages. It is hard for a user to get to the bottom of what exactly is going to happen to their address book if they continue through this process. Such a concern is not unfounded; in 2019, Microsoft was criticised for exposing users contacts to the general public in a now defunct feature called 'People You May Know'.[7]

FORCED ENROLMENT

Forced enrolment is a type of forced action that requires a user to register on a website or app before they're allowed to do the thing they set out to do. Sometimes enrolment is inherently needed as part of the service. For example, Facebook wouldn't be able to show you information about your friends and interests unless it knows who you are, and that requires a user account. However, some services don't inherently require you to register an account. For example, e-commerce sites could let you check out as a guest, but they often don't provide this option. This is because forcing you to register means they can capture your contact information and payment details – all of which is extremely valuable in turning you into a repeat customer.

Similarly, forced enrolment gives the business a choke point: a route all users are forced through. This gives them the opportunity to deploy other deceptive patterns to great effect. For example, businesses can use forced enrolment to extract consent from the user for marketing purposes, for ad retargeting purposes, they can sell or share personal data with third parties, and they can send the user data they get from this into 'lookalike audience' marketing tools which make it possible to target non-customers who look like their existing customers (for example, Google,[8] and Facebook[9]).

Forced enrolment by LinkedIn

This case study of forced enrolment by LinkedIn involves a combination of different deceptive patterns. LinkedIn provides a personalised service. Like all other forms of social media and platforms that store personal data, this inherently requires users to register and sign in – it simply wouldn't work otherwise. So it's not at fault for employing forced enrolment in itself. However, in the earlier days of LinkedIn, it used the enrolment process to force various other actions on users.

In 2015, a class action lawsuit brought to light the deceptive patterns being used by LinkedIn. In a nutshell, LinkedIn was using deceptive patterns to trick users, getting them to upload contacts' email addresses and agreeing to send numerous emails to those individuals, inviting them to join LinkedIn. Some versions of those emails were presented as though they'd been written by the user.

Under California law, this was deemed illegal. LinkedIn was instructed to pay a settlement of $13 million[10]. Dan Schlosser included a detailed walkthrough of the deceptive patterns used in this case, in his 2015 article 'LinkedIn Dark Patterns'.[11] A point worth noting in particular is the second step in the sign-up process:

Grow your network on LinkedIn.   Step **2** of 7 ▰▰▱▱▱

Get started by adding your email address.

Your email: daniinkedintest@gmail.com

Continue

🔒 We'll import your address book to suggest connections and
help you manage your contacts. Learn More

Skip this step »

A deceptive pattern used in LinkedIn's 'Add connections' step during the
forced enrolment process (Schlosser, 2015).

Here, users were asked to enter their email address. As this is a normal
request for most online services, it's unlikely to have been closely scrutinised by users – typing our email address into a field is something we
all do, day in, day out. However, in the words of Dan Schlosser, 'It's
really a lie. This page is not for "adding your email address", it's for
linking address books.' If the user then went on to complete this step
without pressing the small, easy to miss 'Skip this step' link, LinkedIn
then gained access to the user's email contacts via an OAuth dialog.

Having extracted all the email addresses, LinkedIn then sent out
numerous emails to those contracts, inviting them to join the platform.
Overall, this forced enrolment can be considered to be a form of 'friend
spam' where the product asks for your social media or email creden-
tials for an allegedly benign purpose (e.g. finding friends who are
already using that service), but then goes on to publish content or send
out bulk messages using your account, typically impersonating you as
the sender.[12]

CHAPTER 21
HOW DECEPTIVE PATTERNS CAN BE MORE HARMFUL WHEN COMBINED

In 2021, Lior Strahilevitz, a law professor at the University of Chicago, and Jamie Luguri, a PhD in experimental social psychology, came up with a clever way to investigate the quantitative impact of deceptive patterns. They created an online survey that had deceptive patterns in the final section. The main part of the survey was about privacy, but these were all decoy questions, acting as a prelude to the deceptive pattern that would appear near the end.

Strahilevitz and Luguri created a number of different versions of the survey: a control version without any deceptive patterns; a 'mild' dark pattern version; and an 'aggressive' deceptive pattern version. You can see the control and mild versions in the figures below. I haven't included the aggressive version here because it's so bulky. If you're interested to read more, you can refer to their 2021 paper, 'Shining a Light on Dark Patterns'.[1]

CONTROL CONDITION

Using the demographic information you provided at the beginning of the survey and your IP address, we have pinpointed your mailing address. We have partnered with the nation's largest and most experienced data security and identity theft protection company. They will be provided with your answers on this survey. After identifying you, **you will receive six months of data protection and credit history monitoring free of charge**. After the six month period, **you will be billed $8.99 per month** for continued data protection and credit history monitoring. You can cancel this service at any time.

○ Accept

○ Decline

Image depicting a question from the control condition of the Luguri and Strahilevitz study (2021).

In their study, the control condition asks the user if they want to sign up for a 'data protection and credit history monitoring' service that costs $8.99 a month after a free trial period. The user can then either accept or decline without any funny business – there are no deceptive patterns at work.

The mild deceptive pattern makes things a bit more difficult for the user, as shown in the figures below.

"MILD DARK PATTERN" CONDITION

Using the demographic information you provided at the beginning of the survey and your IP address, we have pinpointed your mailing address. We have partnered with the nation's largest and most experienced data security and identity theft protection company. They will be provided with your answers on this survey. After identifying you, **you will receive six months of data protection and credit history monitoring free of charge**. After the six month period, **you will be billed $8.99 per month** for continued data protection and credit history monitoring. You can cancel this service at any time.

○ **Accept and continue (recommended)**

○ Other options

Mild condition 1/3, Luguri and Strahilevitz (2021).

SHOWN IF USER SELECTS "OTHER OPTIONS":

Other options:

○ I do not want to protect my data or credit history

○ After reviewing my options, I would like to protect my privacy and receive data protection and credit history monitoring

Mild condition 2/3, Luguri and Strahilevitz (2021).

SHOWN IF USER SELECTS "I DO NOT WANT TO PROTECT":

Please tell us why you decided to decline this valuable protection.

○ My credit rating is already bad

○ Even though 16.7 million Americans were victimized by identity
theft last year, I do not believe it could happen to me or my family

○ I'm already paying for identity theft and credit monitoring service

○ I've got nothing to hide so if hackers gain access to my data I
won't be harmed

○ Other (minimum 40 characters):

○ On second thought, please sign me up for 6 months of free credit
history monitoring and data protection services

Mild condition 3/3, Luguri and Strahilevitz (2021).

To summarise, in the mild deceptive pattern condition the user is
initially given the same paragraph of text, but they can then pick either
'Accept and continue (recommended)', which is highlighted in bold; or
they can pick 'Other options'. Picking 'Other options' takes them to
another step with more radio buttons. If they try to opt out again ('I do
not want to protect my data or credit history'), they are taken to yet
another step. This design contains a range of different deceptive
patterns: visual interference, trick wording and obstruction. The
aggressive deceptive pattern condition is similar, except it has even
more steps and lays on even more pressure. The aggressive version
also has a countdown timer that forces users to dwell on the subsequent pages, so they can't just skip through quickly.

The researchers deployed this survey to 1,963 participants. The scale of
the impact was staggering:[2]

'**users exposed to mild dark patterns were more than twice as likely to sign up** for a dubious service as those assigned to the control group, and **users in the aggressive dark pattern condition were almost four times as likely to subscribe**.'

— LUGIRI AND STRAHILEVITZ (2021)

Strahilevitz also concluded that 'It's the mild dark patterns that are most insidious' because 'They significantly increased acceptance of a program with dubious benefits without alienating consumers or causing large numbers of them to log off.'[3]

This is an important point. When companies use deceptive patterns, they often don't particularly want to draw attention to their actions from anyone – whether it's their users, consumer action groups, regulators or enforcers.

PART FOUR
HARMS CAUSED BY DECEPTIVE PATTERNS

Deceptive patterns are very common. A 2022 research project by the European Council found that 97% of the websites and apps reviewed contained at least one deceptive pattern[1]. In Chile, a 2021 research project by the National Consumer Service of Chile, SERNAC, found that 64% of the e-commerce websites reviewed had deceptive patterns.[2] In the United States, a 2019 research project by Moser et al. found that 75% of the e-commerce websites reviewed had at least sixteen features that encourage impulse buying.[3] In 2020, Soe et al. analysed the cookie consent notices of 300 news and magazine websites from Denmark, Norway, Sweden, UK and USA. They found that 99% of them used deceptive patterns.[4] In 2023, the EC and CPC network published a report that documented a sweep of 399 online shops and 102 apps; they found that 148 of the online shops (37%) and 27 of the apps (26%) contained deceptive patterns.[5] The evidence is overwhelming, but if you want more, you can view a comprehensive table of further evidence in Annex C of the OECD report 'Dark Commercial Patterns'.[6]

So, it's clear they are widespread, but what kinds of harm do they actually cause? When you think about deceptive patterns from your own personal perspective, the first thing you might think of is the emotional impact, feelings like annoyance and frustration. Although it's normal to respond in this way, there are usually other, even bigger negative consequences to bear in mind. You can look at the harm from different perspectives: harm to individuals; harm to groups in society; and harm to the marketplace.[7]

CHAPTER 22
HARM TO INDIVIDUALS

FINANCIAL LOSS

There are a number of ways a user can suffer financially from deceptive patterns. They might be tricked into making a purchase they didn't intend (sneaking), or they might struggle to cancel a subscription and pay for extra periods without wanting to (hard to cancel). They may also be charged extra fees at the last minute that they did not expect (hidden costs). In a survey of over 2,000 British adults, UK advocacy group Citizens Advice found that respondents lost £50–100 a year on unwanted subscriptions they should not have been charged for.[1]

Another way to look at the scale of financial loss is to look at legal case outcomes, since the size of a fine or settlement typically corresponds with the scale of the financial harm to consumers. At the time of writing, the *deceptive.design* website lists roughly fifty cases where the outcome involves fines or settlements, some of which run into tens of millions of dollars.[2]

TIME LOSS

Everyone has a finite amount of time alive, and deceptive patterns often serve to take it away unfairly. This can happen by making actions difficult (hard to cancel, for instance), by purposefully depleting user's time in order to wear them down (resource depletion), or by making users jump through hoops before they can rectify the outcomes of deceptive patterns, like claiming a refund.

The FTC takes time loss seriously. In a 2022 complaint against credit services company Credit Karma, the FTC argued that Credit Karma's false claims meant 'numerous consumers wasted significant time applying for credit card offers'. They reached a settlement including $3 million in consumer redress, a commitment to stop deceiving consumers, and to preserve design and research records for future investigations.

UNINTENDED CONTRACTS

If a user purportedly enters a legal agreement without being aware that it exists (sneaking), then they may be surprised when the business tries to tie them into it.[3] For example, a mandatory arbitration clause might take away the user's ability to take the business to court.

PRIVACY LOSS

People often don't know their private data is being used without their permission because they can't see it happening. This means that people are often reliant on advocacy groups and other informed parties to fight on their behalf.[4] In 2022, SERNAC carried out a study on over 70,000 users, finding that deceptive patterns can cause substantial privacy loss. By simply changing the default option (opted in to cookies versus opted out), this caused 94 percentage points more users to allow privacy loss to occur.[5]

PSYCHOLOGICAL HARMS

Deceptive patterns often employ psychological techniques to make users emotionally uncomfortable (confirmshaming and pressure selling). In 2019, UK-based researcher Simon Shaw carried out a survey of 2,102 British participants, showing them pages from hotel booking sites that contained pressure selling techniques (scarcity and social proof), and found that 34% of respondents expressed a negative emotion such as contempt or disgust.[6] In 2002, the Australian Consumer Policy Research Center (CPRC) surveyed 2,000 people and found that 40% of them felt annoyed and 28% felt manipulated when a website or app used a deceptive pattern. Similarly, a 2022 European Commission study found that some deceptive patterns led to increases in heart rate and erratic mouse clicks, potentially indicating anxiety.[7]

LOSS OF FREEDOM TO THINK

Human rights lawyer Susie Alegre explains this issue in her book *Freedom to Think*, inspired by the Cambridge Analytica scandal in 2017, which highlighted the use of political behavioural microtargeting on social media to manipulate people.[8] Deceptive patterns play a role in this: enabling social media businesses to extract fake consent from users regarding the use of their personal data; and enabling them to use principles of addiction to make their products so compelling that they can dominate users' consumption of news and understanding of the world at large. Alegre emphasises that this goes beyond privacy and data protection, but rather to the heart of ideological freedom. She explains:[9]

'The rights to freedom of thought, conscience, religion and belief and freedom of opinion are absolute rights protected in international law. Without freedom of thought or opinion, we have no humanity, and we have no democracy. Making these rights real requires three things: (i) the ability to keep your thoughts private;

(ii) freedom from manipulation of your thoughts; (iii) that no one can be penalised for their thoughts alone.'

Given that deceptive patterns directly involve the manipulation of thought, it is clear that they are a central issue in the battle for the human right of freedom of thought, harming not just individuals but society as a whole.[10]

CHAPTER 23
HARM TO GROUPS IN SOCIETY

If we zoom out to a societal level, an important impact of deceptive patterns is that they target some groups in society much more than others – vulnerable groups. This is particularly problematic because those who suffer most often are not in a position to speak up about it, so it can be rather hidden. The disparate impacts on vulnerable groups also makes this an equity issue, exacerbating the problems they already face in life.

Broadly speaking, most deceptive patterns operate by exploiting human cognitive limitations. This means that people who have greater cognitive limitations are more vulnerable than others. Here are some of the types of vulnerable groups that are impacted by deceptive patterns.

PEOPLE WHO SUFFER FROM TIME POVERTY

If someone doesn't have time to read things and carefully apply their critical thinking skills, they're more likely to be caught out by a deceptive pattern. Then, if they are caught out, they need to find the time to complain, return items, get a refund, or rectify the problem in some way. Consider the difference between a wealthy individual who has a four-day working week and no dependents, and a low-income parent who works three jobs and has to care for their three young kids and a sick elderly parent. It's quite obvious that if they realise they are caught out by a deceptive pattern, the first individual will much more easily find the time to remedy the situation, while the latter may never find the time, and might have to simply swallow the loss.

PEOPLE WITH LOW EDUCATION LEVELS

Deceptive patterns work by targeting our perception, comprehension and decision-making capabilities. If someone is not good at dealing with complex sentences or numbers, they have to place their trust in the website or app, which makes them very vulnerable to manipulation. In 2021, researchers Lugiri and Strahilevitz carried out a series of experiments involving 3,932 participants, and found that the less-educated individuals were significantly more susceptible to mild deceptive patterns than their well-educated counterparts.[1]

PEOPLE WITH LOW INCOME

In their 2022 staff report, the FTC argued that people with low income may use mobile devices as their primary means of accessing the internet.[2] The small screens on these devices cause information to be hidden, necessitating a large amount of scrolling, making these users vulnerable to deceptive patterns. The report explains: 'such dark patterns may have a differential impact on lower-income consumers or other vulnerable populations who are more likely to rely on a mobile device as their sole or primary access to the internet.'

SECOND LANGUAGE LEARNERS

After someone migrates to a new country, it can take them a while before they learn the local language fluently, and some people don't ever become proficient. Most countries have citizens who use many different languages. The less common languages are often not well supported by businesses or governments. If someone uses a less common language and is not yet fluent in their country's first language, they become isolated and vulnerable.

PEOPLE WITH COGNITIVE DISABILITIES

Individuals with cognitive disabilities often rely on trusted helpers to manage their affairs since they are unable to perform complex reasoning and decision-making activities on their own. However, sometimes they do not have this help, and that makes them vulnerable.

YOUNG AND OLD PEOPLE

Since children have not yet reached cognitive maturity, and older people often suffer from cognitive decline, they make easy targets for manipulation and deception. For example, in a 2011 study of fraud victims, AARP found that the average age of victims of investment fraud was 69 years old, and victims of lottery fraud was 72 years old.[3] Although it's common for legal safeguards to exist for these groups, this may not be enough to help them avoid deceptive patterns.

CONTEXTUAL VULNERABILITY

Although not strictly a group in the sense used above, we all become more vulnerable in certain situations. For example, you'll perform better in a test if you have slept well and you're able to concentrate. The same applies to dealing with exploitative content that does not have your best interests in mind. Real life is full of compromising contexts. Doing an activity while holding a crying baby in one arm, or while on a bumpy bus ride home after a fourteen-hour shift means that you become distracted and tired, so your cognitive capabilities drop and you will become more vulnerable.

CHAPTER 24
HARM TO THE MARKETPLACE

A healthy marketplace allows consumers to freely choose from a range of competitors and pick the services or products they feel are best suited to their needs. This includes:

- **Competition:** When there are multiple sellers offering similar goods and services, competition encourages them to improve their products, lower prices and innovate in order to attract consumers. Without competition, a small number of sellers can dominate the market, reducing their incentive to improve products, lower prices or innovate.[OBJ]
- **Information symmetry:** Consumers need to know pertinent information about the offerings on the market, so they can make an informed decision. As economist George Akerlof described in 1970, this enables buyers to distinguish good products ('cherries') from bad ones ('lemons'), which thereby reduces the number of lemon providers in the marketplace because consumers choose not to use them.[OBJ]
- **Consumer autonomy:** Consumers need to be free to act on the information they're given in the marketplace, and make decisions based on their preferences, needs and financial resources without being interfered with.[OBJ]

Deceptive patterns can interfere with all of the above characteristics, creating an unhealthy marketplace that can enable monopolies. Put simply, if a business uses deceptive patterns, they put themselves at an advantage over those that do not.

- **Hindering shopping around and comparison:** Businesses can design their offerings and pricing so that consumers find it hard to make comparisons with the competition (by using hidden costs, for instance, or trick wording). This means consumers can't make an informed decision about which provider to select, and they may be tricked into a choice that is not in their best interests.
- **Lock-in to existing services:** Businesses can make it difficult for consumers to leave. For example, the business might have proprietary data formats that make it difficult for a consumer to take their data elsewhere; or they might have proprietary hardware formats that are not compatible with the competition, so that if a consumer wants to leave, they'll have to throw away the hardware they've bought and start again, which they might not be able to afford.
- **Hard to cancel subscriptions:** If a consumer wants to cancel a subscription but can't work out how, the business is effectively trapping them against their will. This effectively starves competing businesses of the income they might otherwise gain from consumers switching providers.

PART FIVE
STAMPING OUT DECEPTIVE PATTERNS

The fact that deceptive patterns haven't gone away or reduced in volume in recent years means that whatever we've tried so far isn't working. It would have been nice to have seen success in some countries or legal jurisdictions so we could look closely at what they've done, but sadly the story is pretty similar worldwide.

When I first wrote about deceptive patterns in 2010, I naively hoped that the problem was mainly around lack of awareness. I hoped that techniques like education, codes of ethics, naming and shaming, and self-regulation would be enough. Given how deceptive patterns are now substantially more widespread than ever before, it's obvious that these approaches aren't working on their own.

CHAPTER 25
OUR ATTEMPTS SO FAR HAVE NOT BEEN SUCCESSFUL

CODES OF ETHICS

Today, the ACM,[1] AIGA,[2] APA,[3] UXPA[4] and other industry bodies all have codes of ethics that – either directly or indirectly – forbid deceptive patterns. These codes of ethics provide standards to aim for, but we are nowhere near meeting them. Codes of ethics are generally ignored by the tech industry, despite our best efforts.

In Europe, article 5 of the Unfair Commercial Practices Directive (UCPD) states that a commercial practice is unfair if it distorts the behaviour of consumers and is 'contrary to the requirements of professional diligence'.[5] The UCPD Guidance goes on to state that the notion of professional diligence 'may include principles derived from national and international standards and codes of conduct'.[6] This means that codes of ethics may become a powerful instrument in preventing deceptive patterns in the EU. However, this hasn't been applied in practice yet, so it's hard to say how it will play out. If one day there is a judicial decision that interprets codes of ethics as 'the requirements of professional diligence' under UCPD article 5 then it will be a game changer and they'll suddenly become enormously important in the fight against deceptive patterns.

Today, businesses often use codes of ethics as a form of 'ethics washing'. It's commonplace to see the message 'We care about your privacy' on a user interface, immediately before they trick you into letting them track you and sell your personal data.

EDUCATION

Education plays a vital role in raising awareness and equipping people with the knowledge to recognize and push back against the use of deceptive patterns. For example, in higher education for design and HCI, it's commonplace to be taught about user-centred design, persuasion and design ethics. They are standard options in higher education courses, and they have been for years. Given the proliferation of deceptive patterns today, it's safe to say that it hasn't stopped them from happening. The economic incentives for businesses to continue to use deceptive patterns are just too strong. In other words, education is necessary but not sufficient. Of course we need education, but we need something more if we're going to solve the problem of deceptive patterns.

BRIGHT PATTERNS

A number of voices have suggested responding to the problem of deceptive patterns with bright patterns[7] or fair patterns[8] – design patterns that are fair towards users. The idea is to fight against deceptive patterns by creating the opposite type of pattern, and then sharing these recommendations as widely as possible.

The sad fact is that we already have a lot of materials that teach designers and business owners how to engage in user-centred or human-centred design processes that result in helpful, usable and useful design patterns that assist users in achieving their goals. Hundreds of university courses, bootcamps and textbooks teach the concepts. There's even an ISO standard on this topic.[9] On their own, bright patterns are really just *yet more educational materials* that appeal to the reader's moral code to do the right thing, which so far hasn't worked.

It's tempting to respond to this by suggesting that perhaps bright patterns should be mandatory. The problem here is the almost infinite variety of design possibilities for any given problem. Consider all the possible configurations of words, images, layouts, buttons and interactive components a design team might want to use – and then also consider all the possible goals they have been asked to bring together. They have their business objectives, various internal stakeholders asking for things, and of course they have to make the thing useful, usable and appealing for end users, otherwise it won't get successfully adopted and used. Then, once the product goes live, it gets iterated. Data is collected from research and analytics, giving clues as to how to make the product more performant. Designs evolve. They're improved, added to, tweaked and trimmed. Design in the digital age is never done, and innovation is an ongoing process.

If you forced the tech industry to use a mandatory bright pattern, you'd stop all of that from happening. You'd kill innovation and improvement overnight. So a regulatorily mandated bright pattern should only be deployed in a very narrow situation – a key juncture when there's a very high risk of harm to users. In fact, this is not a new idea. If you think back to your most recent major financial product (e.g. an investment, loan or mortgage), you were probably given a standardised document that was designed according to regulatory requirements. These documents might not look like much, but they're intended to be bright patterns. The business uses them because they're legally required to, and they serve to help prevent the business from bamboozling you into signing a contract that's against your best interests.

So bright patterns aren't quite as transformative a concept as they initially seem. They're a useful educational tool and they're already mandatory in certain narrow situations, but to stop deceptive patterns we need to go deeper, and look more closely at the business processes and practices that cause them to occur.

NAMING AND SHAMING

Naming and shaming is useful because it can lead to legal consequences. For example, if hundreds of users complain about a provider, this can draw attention from consumer protection groups, regulators and law firms, which can lead to enforcement actions or class action lawsuits.

One of the shortcomings of naming and shaming is that many users don't do it, so the number of complaints can be far smaller than the number of people who have suffered negative consequences. Deceptive patterns are usually designed to be subtle. This means many users don't even know they've suffered negative consequences (perhaps a few dollars for an add-on they didn't intend to buy), so they're not aware they've got anything to complain about. In other words, a very carefully designed deceptive pattern may *never* get named and shamed, because it was so carefully hidden. Also, not everyone wants to speak out publicly – some people are shy or introverted. They might blame themselves for 'being stupid' for being taken in and may feel a sense of shame or embarrassment. If they complain privately to the business, the world never finds out about it (unless the business is forced to reveal it in a legal case). Other people might intend to name and shame, but are unable to find the time. If the consequences are minor (e.g. just a few dollars lost), they might notice and feel irked but not enough to justify the effort of complaining.

All of this means that naming and shaming seems to be effective only for the most noticeable deceptive patterns. It's reasonable to assume that many deceptive patterns never get named and shamed. In summary, naming and shaming is useful, but it's not powerful enough – we need something more.

INDUSTRY SELF-REGULATION

Supporters of industry self-regulation tend to claim that it is faster and more flexible than government regulation, takes advantage of contemporary industry expertise, and reduces administrative burden on governments. Anyone who has been on the receiving end of tedious government bureaucracy knows what bad regulations feel like, so this perspective has some appeal. However, the idea of self-regulation is popular among industry lobbyists because it leaves the door open for superficial gestures and performative compliance, while continuing with whatever profitable practices that went before.

A good example of this is in the European Internet Advertising Bureau's Transparency and Consent Framework (TCF), introduced in 2017.[10] IAB Europe is an industry body that's made up of hundreds of registered companies, advertising vendors and consent management platforms (CMPs) who stand to profit from the ability to track users and show targeted advertisements. At the time, the advertising industry was facing a huge challenge in working out how to deal with the new ePrivacy Directive and GDPR. Put simply, these laws were going to negatively impact profitability in this industry because they required users to explicitly opt in to tracking.[11]

In response, IAB Europe conceived the TCF: a voluntary, industry standard for various things relating to ad-tech, including user consent. This was implemented by numerous CMPs who took the TCF requirements and implemented them in their own user interfaces as 'consent as a service' solutions. These were used at great scale by thousands of website and app owners, seeking to ensure legal compliance.

So how did the CMPs manage to get users to opt in to tracking under the TCF? Simple: they used deceptive patterns extensively. In a research paper on CMPs, Cristiana Santos et al. (2021) explain the motivation:[12]

'The primary service offered by CMPs is to ensure legal compliance [...] However, the advertising industry is also incentivised to strive for maximum consent rates. [...] For example, Quantcast describes their tool as able to *"Protect and maximize ad revenue while supporting compliance with data protection laws"* [...]. OneTrust advertises that its CMP can *"optimize consent rates while ensuring compliance"*, and *"leverage A/B testing to maximize engagement, opt-ins and ad revenue"*.'

You can see the deceptive patterns at work in the series of steps shown below, captured by Soe et al. (2020) in their research paper 'Circumvention by design'.[13] The example depicts a typical cookie wall user interface designed to comply with the TCF v1.0 (the first version of the standard). The option to 'agree' to tracking is a prominent one-click action on every step; while if a user wants to disagree, they have to click 'Learn More' on the first step, then 'Manage partners' on the second step, and then on the third step they have to scroll through a long list of partners, clicking to expand each one and then clicking to opt out of each of them, one by one.

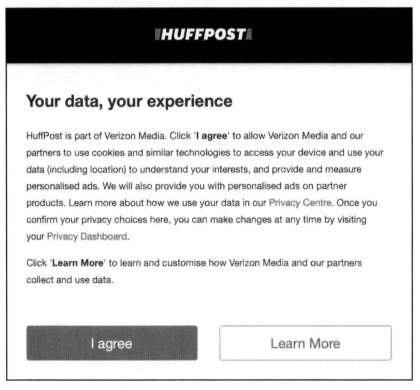

Step 1 of 3. The huffpost.com cookie consent user interface, provided by Yahoo's CMP. It employs various deceptive patterns while being compliant with IAB Europe's TCF 1.0 standard (Soe et al., 2020).

HUFFPOST

How Verizon Media and its partners collect and use data

To continue using Yahoo and other Verizon Media sites and apps, we need you to let us set cookies and similar technologies to collect your data. This helps us improve and create new products, enhance our product security, and give you personalised content and ads. When you let our partners use cookies and similar technologies to collect your data on our sites, they can provide you with ads that match your interests.

Once you confirm your privacy choices here, you can make changes at any time by visiting your Privacy Dashboard.

Select '**I agree**' to proceed or click '**Manage partners**' to manage how our partners use your data.

I agree   Manage partners

Step 2 of 3. Having clicked 'Learn More', the user is still not able to directly reject consent, while they can easily accept it in one click via a big green button labelled 'I agree'. (Soe et al., 2020).

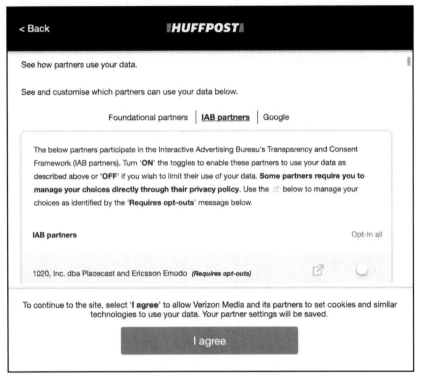

Step 3 of 3. To opt out, the user must scroll through hundreds of partners,
clicking each one to expand it, then clicking a toggle to opt out, one by one.
All the while, they are encouraged to change their mind and skip the ordeal by
consenting via the large green 'I agree' button at the bottom of the window
(Soe et al., 2020).

If you think this example is outrageous, you're not alone. It was eventually found to breach GDPR by the Belgian Data Protection Authority, leading to IAB Europe being fined €250,000 and being required to delete any illegally gathered data.[14] Consumer rights organisation NOYB also filed over 700 complaints regarding TCF and similar designs.

In response, IAB Europe updated the TCF to version 2, in an effort to be more compliant. Even today, privacy researchers are still finding deceptive patterns in CMPs user interfaces under version 2.[15] To quote Pat Walshe, data protection officer of Brave Browser, 'Having the IAB in charge of ad standards aka the TCF is like having Dracula in charge of the national blood bank'.[16]

In January 2023, the European Data Protection Board responded to the complaints with a draft decision, largely in support of them, which is good news in the fight against deceptive patterns in privacy. Ala Krinickytė, data protection lawyer at NOYB, said: 'We are very happy that the authorities agreed on the minimum threshold for protections against abusive banners. Cookie banners became the poster child of the GDPR being undermined. We need authorities to take urgent action, to ensure citizens' trust in European privacy laws.'[17]

In summary, this case study provides a perfect example of why voluntary standards and self-regulation often don't lead to effective outcomes – the incentives simply aren't there. Self-regulation is a way to let an industry carry on doing the same profitable thing as before while pretending to adhere to some new rules.

CHAPTER 26
THE CRUCIAL ROLE OF REGULATION

Education and codes of ethics are clearly necessary, but they aren't themselves enough to solve the problem. As long as deceptive patterns are profitable and low-risk, they will continue to be used.

To understand the importance of regulation, we need to put ourselves in the shoes of business owners. CEOs of tech companies don't wake up in the morning saying to themselves, 'I want my company to use more deceptive patterns'. Instead, they want *more growth* and *more profit* – and deceptive patterns are a by-product. Deceptive patterns are actually a rational response to an under-regulated and under-enforced marketplace. After all, if your company can use a simple UI design technique to deliver more profit and you face little chance of penalties, then why wouldn't you do it?

Laws that apply to citizens are usually easy to understand because they're based on simple rules or belief systems that we're taught from childhood – don't steal, don't kill, that sort of thing. Commercial laws and regulations are different; they can be really complex, and the wording can be difficult to interpret.

This means that in-house lawyers have to analyse commercial laws and help their employers make decisions in the face of this ambiguity. This is called 'legal risk management'. There are various fancy methods and tools that companies use to manage risk. The most basic and common is the risk matrix, shown below.

		Severity				
		Insignificant	Minor	Moderate	Major	Catastrophic
	Certain	Medium	High	Very high	Very high	Very high
	Likely	Medium	High	High	Very high	Very high
Probability	Possible	Low	Medium	High	High	Very high
	Unlikely	Low	Low	Medium	High	High
	Low	Low	Low	Low	Medium	Medium

A typical risk matrix, where a probability rating and severity rating are considered in tandem.

Using this sort of risk matrix, in-house lawyers will consider the probability of negative outcomes from using deceptive patterns (how likely they are to be caught) alongside the severity of the outcome (the size of the financial penalty). If the risk level ends up being very high then they'll pass on this information to their employer who will see it as a good reason to cease engaging in those risky practices. Of course, some businesses don't use risk matrixes like this: it's most popular among compliance-focused industries like finance, healthcare or energy; and less so elsewhere, like e-commerce. Still, businesses that ignore legal risks are likely to land themselves in hot water eventually if sufficient regulations exist.

This leads to an important point about enforcement: regulations on their own are not enough. They need to be enforced, so companies see their competitors getting penalised. This will lead to deceptive patterns moving from the low-risk green area of the risk matrix, into the amber and red areas of higher probability and severity.

CHAPTER 27
LEGISLATION IN THE EUROPEAN UNION

THE UNFAIR COMMERCIAL PRACTICES DIRECTIVE

The Unfair Commercial Practices Directive (UCPD)[1] was adopted back in 2005, and it doesn't get talked about much, despite its potency. It's a bit like the elderly grey-haired character in a martial arts movie whom everyone ignores, but in the third act they turn out to be a total power-house who packs an incredible punch.

The UCPD applies to all business-to-commercial practices in the EU and UK.[2] It covers almost any decision that a consumer has to make while using a digital service or in a physical store. This includes decisions made before a commercial transaction, during it, or after. So that means it covers marketing, advertising, personalisation, choice architecture, and deceptive patterns (although deceptive patterns aren't explicitly defined in the law). The UCPD also doesn't require intent, so if a design is shown to be unfair, that's good enough – it doesn't need proof that the designers or business owners created it on purpose.

The UCPD contains a number of principles:

- **General prohibition of unfair commercial practices:** The UCPD prohibits any commercial practice that is contrary to the requirements of professional diligence and materially distorts or is likely to distort the economic behaviour of the average consumer.

- **Misleading practices**: The UCPD prohibits misleading actions and omissions, which involve providing false information or presenting information in a way that deceives or is likely to deceive the average consumer. This includes misleading advertising, false claims about products or services, and other deceptive tactics.
- **Aggressive practices:** The UCPD prohibits aggressive commercial practices, which significantly impair the average consumer's freedom of choice or conduct through harassment, coercion, or undue influence. This includes high-pressure sales tactics, persistent and unwanted solicitations, and exploiting a consumer's vulnerability or fear.

'Professional diligence' is noteworthy because it implies that if an organisation ignores a widely used set of professional conduct guidelines, this could fall under the prohibition. Most of these sorts of guidelines contain provisions about deceptive patterns, either directly or indirectly, such as the ACM's Code of Ethics and Professional Conduct.[3] The UCPD also contains a list of forbidden practices ('Annex 1: Commercial practices which are in all circumstances considered unfair'). This is probably the most powerful weapon in the UCPD's arsenal, because it's so easy to use. The regulator doesn't have to carry out a detailed analysis that proves deception occurred. All they have to do is show that the banned practice was used by the business, and that's that. There are 31 forbidden practices. Here's a summary of the most relevant ones:

- (2) **Fake trust markers**: falsely displaying a trust mark, quality mark or similar.
- (4) **Fake endorsements**: falsely claiming a trader or product has an endorsement approved, endorsed or authorised by a public or private body.

- (5) **Bait advertising**: advertising a certain price when the trader knows they cannot offer that product, or only has a few in stock at that price.
- (6) **Bait and switch**: advertising a product at a certain price then refusing to offer it, with the intention of promoting a different product.
- (7) **Fake urgency**: falsely stating that a product or terms will only be available for a very limited time, to rush the user and deprive them of the time to make an informed choice.
- (11) **Covert advertising**: presenting paid advertorial without disclosing that it is an advertisement.
- (20) **Fake free offers**: describing something as free when it's not.
- (21) **Fake invoices**: claiming the user owes a bill when they do not.

In summary, with a combination of the principles and the forbidden practices, the UCPD covers a lot of deceptive patterns – which is really good news. However, the UCPD's main strength is also its shortcoming. It has an extremely broad scope: if a company engages in a practice that isn't an exact fit for one of the forbidden practices, then the legal case has to provide a detailed argument regarding how the practice violates the UCPD's principles (such as, that it's unfair, misleading or aggressive towards an 'average consumer'). Consumer protection litigation is naturally very slow. The broad scope of the UCPD is unlikely to help speed it up.

THE GENERAL DATA PROTECTION REGULATION

The General Data Protection Regulation (GDPR)[4] protects the data of individuals. It forbids certain deceptive patterns that fall within the realm of data and privacy.

- **Data protection by design and default**: Under article 25 of GDPR, designers must ensure that the implementation of the 'data protection by design and default' principle is not impacted by deceptive patterns. For example, a user interface cannot be designed to have a data-intrusive option as the default, nor can it obscure settings through the use of misdirection (such as visual interference or trick wording). Article 25 also forbids the use of nagging or persistent pestering to manipulate users into giving up their data protection rights.

- **Consent indication**: GDPR contains a prohibition on the processing of personal data. Businesses cannot do it unless they follow the rules. One of these rules is to be able to have a legal basis or grounds for the processing of personal data. There are only six grounds for processing personal data, one of which is consent-based. Businesses must also comply with the data protection principles, like fairness, data minimization, accuracy and transparency. Consent gets a lot of attention because it has historically been the easiest to get. However, GDPR raised the consent threshold to the high threshold of 'freely given, specific, informed, and unambiguous'. Deceptive patterns compromise the transparency principle and the legal standard required to show consent.
- **Transparency principle**: Under article 5(1)(a) of GDPR, businesses must ensure that they process data in a 'transparent manner', which means means they must communicate to users about their proposed data processing using clear and intelligible language – deceptive patterns are forbidden if they interfere with this.

In summary, if a business uses a deceptive pattern relating to personal data, and the user is an EU or UK citizen, then it's likely to be forbidden under GDPR. The fines can be very severe, which is one of the reasons why business owners pay such close attention to it – up to €20 million, or up to 4% of the annual worldwide turnover, whichever is greater.

THE CONSUMER RIGHTS DIRECTIVE

The Consumer Rights Directive (CRD)[5] was introduced in 2014 to harmonise consumer protection rules and ensure that consumers have a high level of protection across the EU member states. While the CRD does not explicitly mention deceptive patterns, it does contain a number provisions that address them. For example:

- **Information requirements** (articles 5 and 6): The CRD mandates that businesses (termed 'traders' in the CRD) must provide consumers with clear and comprehensible information about the main characteristics of a product or service, its price and additional charges. This can be used to regulate deceptive patterns that involve hiding or obscuring essential information, making it difficult for consumers to make informed decisions.
- **Right of withdrawal** (article 9): The CRD grants consumers a fourteen-day right of withdrawal for distance and off-premises contracts. This can be used as a safety net, to counteract deceptive patterns that trick users into making purchases or entering contracts without fully understanding the implications.
- **Pre-ticked boxes** (article 22): The CRD explicitly prohibits the use of pre-ticked boxes for additional payments – known as the sneaking or 'sneak into basket' deceptive pattern. This is commonly employed to increase revenue by adding extra products or services without the explicit consent of the consumer. Businesses must seek active consent from consumers for any additional payments.
- **Prohibition of inertia selling** (article 27): The CRD prohibits the practice of sending unsolicited goods or services to consumers and then demanding payment for them. In other words, businesses are not allowed to send products to consumers without their explicit request and then ask for payment. Consumers are not required to pay for or return such unsolicited goods.

- **Contract terms** (article 3): The CRD requires that contract terms and conditions must be communicated to consumers in plain and intelligible language. This provision can be helpful in addressing deceptive patterns that use complex or confusing language to deceive or manipulate users into agreeing to unfavourable terms.
- **Additional charges and fees** (article 19): The CRD requires traders to clearly and prominently disclose any additional fees or charges before the consumer is bound by the contract. This provision can help regulate deceptive patterns that involve hidden fees or charges, which are added without the user's knowledge or consent.

These provisions in the Consumer Rights Directive, among others, aim to provide a fair and transparent marketplace for consumers. While the CRD does not explicitly target deceptive patterns, its focus on consumer protection means that it can be used to address them.

OTHER EU LAWS

In general, if a deceptive pattern is used to avoid legal obligations or deceive consumers in a way that violates existing laws or regulations, it is usually going to be considered illegal. This means that there are quite a few other laws and regulations that indirectly forbid deceptive patterns. For example:

- **UCTD** (1993): The Unfair Contract Terms Directive[6] requires that all contracts between users and businesses must be fair and reasonable. It also has a transparency requirement (article 5) that requires all contracts to be drafted in plain and intelligible language.
- **AVMSD** (2018): The Audiovisual Media Services Directive[7] contains a number of provisions that aim to protect viewers. This includes the protection of minors and a requirement of transparency regarding advertising, sponsorship and product placement.

- **E-commerce Directive** (2000): This directive contains a number of provisions that aim to protect e-commerce consumers[8]. For example, providers must clearly identify themselves, provide contact details (article 5), the terms of promotional offers must be clearly stated (article 6) and advertisements must be unambiguously labelled.
- **ePrivacy Directive** (2002): This Directive seeks to protect the privacy and confidentiality of users' electronic communications[9]. There is some overlap with GDPR, which is a newer and broader directive. ePrivacy has some provisions that indirectly protect against deceptive patterns. For example, it requires users to be provided with clear and comprehensive information about the use of cookies and similar tracking technologies and be given the opportunity to refuse them (article 5(3)). It also forbids spam, requiring that users provide their explicit consent before receiving commercial communications. Deceptive patterns cannot be used to circumvent these provisions.

These EU laws are enforced by various regulatory authorities and bodies, typically at a national level. In some industries, the regulators create additional rules to improve consumer protection and prevent deceptive patterns. For example, industries that involve complex services, information asymmetries, or that have been prone to market failures in the past (like financial services or telecommunications). These additional rules can be in the form of guidelines, recommendations, or even specific regulations at the national level.

In addition to this, individuals and sometimes groups of citizens can file lawsuits against companies that operate in the EU, although group action (aka class action) is far more common in the US because of different systems, cultural norms and economic factors.

CHAPTER 28
LEGISLATION IN THE UNITED STATES

Like the EU, the United States also has a number of existing laws that cover deceptive patterns. In a 2022 staff report, the FTC stated that it intends to take action against companies that use deceptive patterns when they violate the FTC Act, ROSCA, TSR, TILA, CAN-SPAM, COPPA, ECOA (plus other statutes and regulations).[1] These are the main federal laws that the FTC sees as relevant to deceptive patterns.

THE FEDERAL TRADE COMMISSION ACT

The Federal Trade Commission (FTC) Act doesn't mention anything about deceptive patterns, but that's because it was enacted over a hundred years ago in 1914. Even so, it has lots of good stuff in it that prohibits unfair or deceptive practices in commerce, and so it can be used to address deceptive patterns indirectly. This law also established the FTC as the agency responsible for enforcing the law. Much of the FTC's work is done under section 5 of the FTC Act which prevents unfair and deceptive acts and practices. The test for unfairness consists of three elements:

- **Substantial injury**: The practice causes harm to consumers, or is likely to do so.

- **Not reasonably avoidable**: The injury must not be reasonably avoidable by consumers.
- **Not outweighed by benefits:** The injury must not be outweighed by countervailing benefits to consumers or competition.

In the words of former FTC commissioner Rebecca Slaughter at the Computers, Privacy and Data Protection conference in 2022[2]: 'That is a complicated test… That's why we've used [the provisions for] deception more, because it is an easier test to meet!' The deception test is simpler, which Slaughter cheerfully summarises as 'Don't lie about what you're doing – with data or otherwise – or we will sue you'. The deception test consists of three elements:

- **Representation, omission, or practice**: There must be a representation, omission, or practice that is likely to mislead the consumer.
- **Reasonable consumer**: The representation, omission, or practice must be examined from the perspective of a reasonable consumer in the given circumstances.
- **Materiality**: The misleading representation, omission, or practice must be material, meaning it is likely to affect the consumer's decision regarding the product or service.

To summarise: by applying the tests for deception or unfairness, the FTC can investigate and take enforcement actions against businesses using deceptive patterns that mislead or harm consumers, thus protecting consumers and promoting fair competition.

OTHER US FEDERAL LAWS

A number of other federal laws indirectly relate to deceptive patterns. For example:

- **ECOA** (1974): Equal Credit Opportunity Act is a federal law that prohibits lenders from discriminating against borrowers on the basis of race, colour, national origin, religion, sex, marital status, age, or receipt of public assistance. The ECOA does not cover deceptive patterns directly, but it is possible for deceptive patterns to be used in a manner that is covered by this law, such as misdirection or hidden costs in loan or credit application forms.

- **COPPA** (1998): Children's Online Privacy Protection Act is a federal law that requires websites and online services to obtain parental consent before collecting personal information from children under the age of 13. COPPA does not cover deceptive patterns directly, but it is applicable when deceptive patterns are used to violate its rules, such as misdirection to falsely achieve parental consent, or other tricks and traps that impact children's privacy.

- **ROSCA** (2010): Restore Online Shoppers' Confidence Act is a federal law that requires online merchants to obtain a customer's express informed consent before charging them for goods or services. It contains two provisions regarding the hard to cancel deceptive pattern (which it refers to as deceptive or unfair 'negative option' subscription practices). Specifically, all terms of the subscription – including renewal frequency and price – must be clearly and conspicuously disclosed to the customer before obtaining the consumer's billing information (they can't be tricked into a subscription); and a provider must offer a simple mechanism to cancel a negative option subscription.

- **CAN-SPAM** (2003): Controlling the Assault of Non-Solicited Pornography and Marketing Act is a federal law that prohibits deceptive email marketing practices. It requires companies to obtain consent from users before sending them commercial emails. It also includes not sending misleading emails, providing a way for users to opt out of future emails, and honouring opt-out requests promptly. CAN-SPAM doesn't cover deceptive patterns directly, but it is applicable when deceptive patterns are used to violate any of these rules.

- **TSR** (1994): Telemarketing Sales Rule is a federal law that regulates telemarketing activities. It prohibits deceptive telemarketing practices and sets standards for how businesses may contact customers via phone. Although CSR doesn't cover deceptive patterns directly, it is applicable when deceptive patterns are used to violate any of TSR's rules.
- **TILA** (1968): Truth in Lending Act is a federal law that requires lenders to disclose important information about the terms of a loan to borrowers. This includes the interest rate, loan fees, the total cost of the loan, and the total amount the borrower will have to pay back. Lenders that use deceptive patterns in order to deceive or mislead consumers may be in violation of TILA.

OTHER US STATE LAWS

The US also has state laws, though federal law takes precedence over state law in case of conflicts. Most states have laws that relate to consumer protection that could potentially be invoked in legal disputes concerning deceptive patterns. Here are a few of them.

- **California Privacy Rights Act**: The CPRA builds on the California Consumer Privacy Act (CCPA) and includes specific provisions addressing 'dark patterns'. It requires businesses to provide clear and comprehensible choices for consumers regarding the collection, use, and sharing of their personal information. The law explicitly prohibits the use of 'dark patterns' that have the substantial effect of subverting or impairing a consumer's choice to opt out of the sale or sharing of their personal information. The CPRA also establishes the California Privacy Protection Agency (CPPA), which is responsible for enforcing the law.
- **Colorado Privacy Act (Senate Bill 21-190)**: The CPA aims to enhance consumer privacy by offering individuals greater control over their personal data collected and processed by businesses. The act defines and regulates 'dark patterns', but only in the context of consent for the processing of personal

data. It stipulates that businesses must not employ 'dark patterns' when responding to consumers' opt-out requests.

- **New York General Business Law**: New York's GBL protects consumers from deceptive acts and practices under article 22-A, titled 'Consumer Protection from Deceptive Acts and Practices.' Specifically, Section 349 prohibits deceptive acts or practices in the conduct of any business, trade, or commerce, or in the furnishing of any service. The law does not specifically mention deceptive patterns, but its broad scope could potentially encompass cases involving manipulative or misleading design elements. The New York State Attorney General's Office is responsible for enforcing the GBL.

- **Massachusetts Consumer Protection Act** (MGL C93A): Also known as 'Regulation of Business Practices for Consumers' Protection', this law aims to protect consumers from unfair and deceptive practices in trade or commerce. It covers a wide range of business activities and practices, and its broad language could be applied to cases involving deceptive patterns. It is also rather powerful, providing for double and treble damages in certain circumstances, as well as attorneys' fees and costs (see sections 9a to 9c). The Massachusetts Attorney General's Office is responsible for enforcing this law, and consumers can also file private lawsuits to seek redress.

- **Washington Consumer Protection Act** (RCW 19.86): This Act prohibits unfair or deceptive practices in commerce under its Section 19.86.020. It is a broad law that aims to protect consumers from a wide range of deceptive practices, including those in advertising, sales and services. Although it does not specifically mention deceptive patterns, its provisions could potentially be applied to cases involving deceptive design elements. The Washington State Attorney General's Office is responsible for enforcing this law.

CHAPTER 29
ENFORCEMENT
CHALLENGES

When you look at the pervasiveness of deceptive patterns today, it may seem like today's laws and regulations aren't working, but that's not strictly true. *They're kind of working.* The current state of affairs is a bit like a spluttering kitchen tap with low water pressure – a lot of waiting around and frustration. We are at a transitory point where we have old laws that weren't written with deceptive patterns in mind, and new laws coming in that haven't fully bedded in yet.

The problem with enforcing consumer law is that it's slow and expensive, even at the best of times. Deceptive patterns are often designed to be subtle and intricate, making them difficult to identify and prove in a legal context. Consumer protection law is complex, and the wording of the law can be ambiguous, leading to battles over interpretation. Then, of course, you've got the differences between the member states: the EU is made up of countries that may have different enforcement strategies; while the US is made up of states that may create their own laws. This creates even more complexity. Let's look at the reasons for slowness more closely.

RESOURCE CONSTRAINTS

To effectively monitor and enforce existing laws, agencies require a combination of technically proficient staff, efficient systems and sufficient personnel. To do this, they need money. Budget allocation comes from politicians who have to make difficult choices about where public money goes. Sometimes agencies just don't get the money they need to do their jobs properly.

QUESTION OF MOTIVATION

Another barrier to effective enforcement of regulations is the lack of motivation in some agencies. For instance, some critics accuse the Irish Data Protection Commissioner of being slow to enforce GDPR. In a 2019 Politico article titled 'How one country blocks the world on data privacy' Nicholas Vinocur scathingly commented, 'Ireland has a long history of catering to the very companies it is supposed to oversee, having wooed top Silicon Valley firms to the Emerald Isle with promises of low taxes, open access to top officials, and help securing funds to build glittering new headquarters'.[1]

In its defence, the Irish Data Protection Commissioner has stepped up the pace recently, fining Meta €390 million in January 2023[2] and then €1.2 billion just a few months later in May.[3] Still, it seems that under-budgeting an agency can potentially be politically motivated. After all, it's understandable that a government might want to attract large international businesses by making the environment more appealing.

NATURE OF PRINCIPLE-BASED LAWS

Consumer protection laws are generally principle-based. This characteristic is a double-edged sword. While it lends these laws the flexibility to adapt to new practices, making them somewhat future-proof, it also inherently slows their responsiveness. Each case has to be meticulously worked through the legal system, a time-consuming process that allows companies to exploit existing loopholes.

FORBIDDEN PRACTICES AND PENALTIES

In the EU, forbidden practices were added to the Unfair Commercial Practices Directive to ban outright certain deceptive patterns (aka a blacklist). This is helpful, but it has only been updated once since it was created in 2005, and it doesn't provide any real detail about punitive measures.[4] This raises the obvious question of whether such an approach would work better if there was a faster way to update the list of forbidden practices, and stronger punitive measures if those practices are used (for example, higher fines).

WHAT IT'S LIKE BEING AN EXPERT WITNESS IN LAWSUITS

Here's a summary of my experience as an expert witness on deceptive patterns in various legal cases in the United States.

First, I get contacted by a law firm. The initial conversations can be quite cryptic – they often don't like putting anything in writing in case a poorly worded off-the-cuff statement gets used against them in the future. Once they've established trust, they tell me what the case is about.

Many of these sorts of law firms spend their time hunting for weaknesses in legal armour, targeting high-value tech companies and searching endlessly for ways in which to find a case that can lead to a payday for them – and relatively little money for the individual plaintiffs. This is rather different to the Hollywood image of class action suits where the story starts with a group of wronged individuals and a plucky lawyer steps up to help them. Still, even though the class action model has downsides, the lure of a big payday for the lawyers attracts many energetic and capable firms to fight on behalf of users, and the threat of these sorts of lawsuits can deter businesses from breaking the law.

In the initial call, I'm typically asked to give my opinion on a few screenshots of a user journey: *'Are there any deceptive patterns at play here?'*, for instance. When my answer is no, the conversation is over and they either go off looking for a different expert or a different case. When my answer is yes or maybe, I get engaged by the law firm. Every case I've worked on so far has started with a preliminary analysis where I capture extensive screenshots of the user journey and look closely at every step using an expert evaluation method.

I typically use a mystery shopper method in which I'll define a persona with certain characteristics and a goal in mind. For example, if it's a sports ticket sales e-commerce journey then the characteristics and goals will relate to sport events. Then I document the steps such a user is likely to go through, taking a screenshot at each step. To use academic HCI terminology, this is a type of lightweight persona-based[5] 'cognitive walkthrough' method,[6] though instead of aiming to evaluate usability, it aims to identify the presence of deceptive patterns, the mechanics of how they work, and the ways in which a reasonable user may experience negative consequences as a result.

In my work I usually capture high-resolution full page screenshots (Firefox has this capability built in[7]) and screen-recording video clips (when animations and transitions are important) and put them all into a visual database tool (there are many alternatives available, including NocoDB,[8] Baserow,[9] and Airtable.[10]) This allows me to store the screenshots along with metadata like date, sequence, user journey, device, and so on. This sort of fastidious approach to documentation is vital because cases can go on for months, or even years (I am working on one case that started in 2019 and is still ongoing in 2023). The work often involves working for a few days, then stopping for a few weeks or months, only to suddenly get a phone call and be back on the clock again. Sometimes I have to go back through the materials with a different frame of analysis, and I wouldn't be able to do that without a readily searchable and filterable database.

This part of the work can be extremely laborious. Since websites and apps are changed frequently, deceptive patterns may be altered, removed or replaced over time. This makes the work almost like archeological excavation – it requires me to locate and identify older versions that are not currently live. Sometimes I start with little more than screenshots from consumer complaints in blog posts or social media. Sometimes I can use the Internet Archive Wayback Machine for evidence, though it only covers the public-facing World Wide Web – it can't index authenticated experiences (if a user has to proceed through registration, login or payment, the Internet Archive is blocked). Sometimes the user journey is different on iOS, Android and desktop native apps. Sometimes websites present information in different ways depending on the viewport size, thanks to the CSS and JavaScript layout rules of the page. Tools like Browserstack Live can be useful for this, allowing you to remotely use and take screenshots from a very wide range of real devices and browsers.[11] This creates a multiplying effect when I may end up having to look at the same user journey over and over again, at different points in time, for different devices and viewport sizes.

Then there is branching and business logic within the user journey itself. For example, I've worked on a few cases where the user is presented with questions or choices, and depending on their responses they are guided towards different products or services. In these situations, the expert may need to reverse engineer how the system works by going through the journey over and over again and documenting the behaviour. Cases that involve complex algorithms (such as personalisation and recommendation systems) typically involve other experts who have experience writing that sort of software.

During a case, the expert can suggest what documents to request from the defendant (for example, during document discovery). In my experience it's useful to ask for feature documentation, analytics reports, A/B test documentation and qualitative user research reports. In some cases, there's an opportunity to suggest who to depose (obtain a sworn testimony) from the defendant's organisation. This can involve looking through the organisational chart and proposing who might be the best source of information when questioned under oath. Lawyers aren't always familiar with how decision-making happens in tech companies. For example, it may look like a data analyst is a good person to depose since they work closely with interesting data, but in reality they're usually far removed from the strategic decision-making. A product manager in the relevant area is usually a better bet, since they are close enough to the details while still being heavily involved in strategic decision-making.

In my experience working as an expert witness, defending companies will cooperate to the extent they are legally required, but no further. For example, in one case, I asked for analytics data relating to traffic from one page to another: I received a spreadsheet containing a single number. In another case, I asked for information about A/B tests performed on a section of a website within a given time period, and received several megabytes of JSON metadata – useless because they were not human-readable and didn't provide any images or descriptions of the user interface designs that were A/B tested. Of course these sorts of issues can be sorted out through further dialogue, but it's time consuming and costly.

After writing an initial analysis and sharing it with legal counsel, it's normal for the expert to submit a signed declaration. Following that, they may be asked to testify in court, where they get cross-examined by the defendant's counsel.

To summarise, expert witness work in this area is very labour-intensive. In fact, the same applies to most legislation and regulations around the world that relate to deceptive patterns – it takes a lot of people, effort and time to carry out this kind of lawsuit.

TECHNOLOGY AS A TOOL

It is hoped that some of the labour of research and analysis will become partially automated or streamlined using technology – a new area known as 'EnfTech' (a portmanteau of enforcement and tech). It's not widely available yet, but here are some of the things that EnfTech should be able to help with.

- **Crawling the web to find evidence in source code**: In the same way that search engines use bots to spider the web and create an index, similar bots can be written to scan the web and find website source code that exhibits characteristics of deceptive patterns. This can then be added to a shortlist of potential cases that can be vetted by human investigators.

- **Scanning social media and review sites to find complaints**: Lots of digital products cannot be seen by web crawlers, and require accounts to access. Luckily, users often complain publicly on social media or review sites. Various products already exist for brands to track social media sentiment, like Brandwatch[12] or Mentionlytics,[13] so it's easy to imagine this sort of technology being applied for tracking complaints about deceptive patterns.

- **Evidence archival**: Once a business is considered worthy of investigation, an agency can use an automated tool to create accounts, manage account states, and take screenshots or capture source code for future reference. These sorts of tools are frequently used internally in businesses for QA and documentation (Selenium[14] for instance, or Air/shots[15]).

- **Issuing automated warnings**: Instead of having a human writing manual emails or letters, a bot can be used to write them and to locate the relevant contact details.

A good example of new EnfTech in practice is NOYB's WeComply.[16] WeComply works by automatically sending GDPR complaints, providing a step-by-step guide on how to remedy the issue, and if the recipient company chooses not to take action, then it files a complaint with the relevant authority. In 2021, *noyb.eu* sent over 500 draft complaints to companies who use unlawful cookie banners (under GDPR).[17]

GDPR violations are a particular kind of highly structured problem that are well suited to automation. Deceptive patterns in general are much broader and harder to pin down – one business's approach to deception will be different to another's. This means EnfTech won't always be able to provide such a high level of automation, but any amount of streamlining is still valuable.

Despite the promise of EnfTech, it doesn't actually change the legislative dynamic that puts an enormous burden of work on the enforcer. In a report arguing for legal reform in the EU, the European Consumer Organisation (BEUC) suggests that we need new rules 'alleviating the burden of proof for plaintiffs and enforcement authorities'.[18] I couldn't agree more.

PART SIX
THE ROAD AHEAD

Deceptive patterns have become a hot topic, both in the tech world capitalising on it, and in the legislative and regulatory world working to bring it under control.

As time has passed, it has become clear that deceptive patterns aren't just a matter of user rights. Although things like unintended financial transactions and privacy infractions are harmful to individuals, it's the consequences to society as a whole that are most worrying.[1] Deceptive patterns disproportionately affect the most vulnerable groups in society, and the companies most willing to use deceptive patterns gain an unfair advantage against any competing companies that have a more ethical or user-centred mission.[2] If left unchecked, the small number of large, powerful monopolies we have today will entrench their power even further. You can imagine how capable such companies will be – their large, hard to monitor platforms together with armies of data scientists, psychologists and designers will create bigger, better breeding grounds for all sorts of new forms of manipulation and deception.

Although deceptive patterns prevent users from making decisions in their own best interests, they are also anti-competitive, making it difficult for companies to compete with those willing to use them. Misdirection can lure users to use a business on false pretences (e.g. deceptive testimonials), and establish false consent and false contractual agreement when they enter a business relationship (selling their personal data or binding them into arbitration agreements). Obstruction can make it hard for users to leave or to take their data with them when they want to migrate to a competitor. All of this means that tech companies aren't just manipulating individuals, they're manipulating the marketplace – and preventing fair competition. Princeton academics Mathur, Mayer and Kshirsagar support this idea, arguing that dominant providers can 'abuse their position of monopoly power and diminish competition by making it look like consumers independently selected their product rather than from a series of dark patterns that disfavor offers from competitors'.[3] Antitrust experts Jay L Himes and Jon Crevier also propose that deceptive patterns create an unfair advantage to first movers and disfavour companies that enter the market later on.[4] Once a first-mover employs deceptive patterns to capture users, drain their attention, and impair their autonomy to leave or shop elsewhere, this increases the cost for rivals to compete.

CHAPTER 30
CHANGES AFOOT IN THE EUROPEAN UNION

The European Union is putting considerable energy into preventing deceptive patterns. Existing legal frameworks like the General Data Protection Regulation and the consumer law frameworks, including the Unfair Commercial Practices Directive, are currently being deployed extensively against platforms that use deceptive patterns. What's more, the EU has been working on two huge new laws that will extensively regulate big tech. By the first quarter of 2024, the Digital Services Act and the Digital Markets Act will have come into force. Both of these laws contain specific provisions regulating deceptive patterns and manipulative design. This is a step forward from the GDPR and the UCPD, which require interpretation and legal application of concepts like consent, transparency, and unfairness to deceptive patterns.

THE DIGITAL MARKETS ACT

The Digital Markets Act (DMA) was created in March 2022 with the goal of ensuring fair and open digital markets in the EU.[1] It targets big tech companies like Microsoft, Apple, Google, Meta and Amazon. Any company that has either more than 45 million monthly active EU users, or over €7.5 billion annual turnover in the EU may be defined as a 'gatekeeper' and is subject to obligations under the DMA. There are also some qualitative criteria that appear to be designed to prevent influential companies from sneaking under the size requirements[2]. In the words of the European Commission, the DMA aims at 'preventing gatekeepers from imposing unfair conditions on businesses and end users and at ensuring the openness of important digital services'.[3]

The DMA bans deceptive patterns when they're used to undermine the *other rules* in the DMA (article 13). The other rules are very wide-ranging, so this means that the DMA is powerful in its scope regarding deceptive patterns. For example, the recitals of the DMA (the part of the legislation that explains how to interpret the provisions) clearly state that deceptive patterns are forbidden if they are used by gatekeepers to do any of the following:

- Interfere with a user's choice to be tracked or not for targeted advertising outside the gatekeeper's main platform (recital 36, 37).
- Nag users; that is, prompt them more than once a year to give consent for data processing, having previously ignored or refused the request (recital 37).
- Interfere with a user's choice to install third-party apps or app stores (recital 41).
- Interfere with a user's choice of settings, or their choice to uninstall any pre-installed apps (recital 49).
- Interfere with a user's ability to export their data from the gatekeeper's platform in a format that can be imported to third parties (recital 59).
- Make it more difficult for a user to unsubscribe from a service than it was to subscribe (recital 63).

This demonstrates how enormously consequential the DMA will be for tech companies that get categorised as gatekeepers. If a gatekeeper breaks the rules, the sanctions are potentially huge: up to 10% of the company's total worldwide annual turnover, or 20% if they are repeat offenders. There are other sanctions possible too, ranging all the way up to having the gatekeeper broken up or kicked out of the EU entirely.

THE DIGITAL SERVICES ACT

The EU Digital Services Act (DSA) contains even more good news about deceptive patterns.[4] It entered into force in November 2022, and is gradually being rolled out, with the parts about deceptive patterns becoming fully applicable by June 2023. The DSA has a layered system with the rules becoming stricter at each successive level.

The DSA contains provisions about deceptive patterns, but they only apply to the two highest tiers: 'online platforms' and – something of a mouthful – 'very large online platforms' and 'very large online search engines' (VLOPs and VLOSEs):

- **Online platforms**: A service 'that, at the request of a recipient of the service, stores and disseminates information to the public'. This includes online marketplaces (like Amazon), app stores (like Apple's App Store and Google Play), collaborative economy platforms (like Uber) and social media platforms (like Facebook).
- **Very large online platforms (VLOPs) and very large online search engines (VLOSEs)**: VLOPs are the same as online platforms, only bigger, with 45+ million monthly active users. VLOSEs are search engines (like Google) that have 45+ million monthly active users.

The DSA's provisions about deceptive patterns don't apply to the lower tiers. So, the following are excluded:

- **Micro and small enterprises**: Any business with a headcount of less than 50 and a turnover of less than €10 million (unless the size of their user base makes them a VLOP or VLOSE).
- **Intermediary services**: Offering network infrastructure – things like VPNs, DNS services, domain name registries, registrars, VOIP services, CDNs, and so on.

- **Hosting services**: Offering cloud and web hosting, such as Godaddy or Amazon Web Services (AWS).

As you can see, the layered nature of the DSA is a bit complicated, but the main point to take away is that the provisions about deceptive patterns apply to lots of big tech companies. Apple, Amazon, Uber, Google, Facebook – they're all regulated by the DSA in some capacity.

Now we've established that, we can move on to the actual provisions in the DSA that regulate deceptive patterns. The term 'dark pattern' is defined in the DSA recitals (recital 67). To quote:

> 'Dark patterns on online interfaces of online platforms are practices that materially distort or impair, either on purpose or in effect, the ability of recipients of the service to make autonomous and informed choices or decisions. Those practices can be used to persuade the recipients of the service to engage in unwanted behaviours or into undesired decisions which have negative consequences for them. Providers of online platforms should therefore be prohibited from deceiving or nudging recipients of the service and from distorting or impairing the autonomy, decision-making, or choice of the recipients of the service via the structure, design or functionalities of an online interface or a part thereof. This should include, but not be limited to, exploitative design choices to direct the recipient to actions that benefit the provider of online platforms, but which may not be in the recipients' interests'

It's notable that the recital states that deceptive patterns do not have to be intentional; they only have to be shown to have an effect on users ('either on purpose or in effect'), which is also the case in the UCPD for unfair commercial practices, and it will make enforcement more straightforward. The recital also goes on to explicitly forbid certain deceptive patterns – though bear in mind that a 'recital' in EU law is not legally binding; it's just intended to clarify the law.

- **Misdirection**: 'presenting choices in a non-neutral manner, such as giving more prominence to certain choices through visual, auditory, or other components, when asking the recipient of the service for a decision'.
- **Nagging:** 'It should also include repeatedly requesting a recipient of the service to make a choice where such a choice has already been made'.
- **Hard to cancel:** 'making the procedure of cancelling a service significantly more cumbersome than signing up to it, or making certain choices more difficult or time-consuming than others, making it unreasonably difficult to discontinue purchases'.
- **Obstruction:** 'default settings that are very difficult to change, and so unreasonably bias the decision making of the recipient of the service, in a way that distorts and impairs their autonomy, decision-making and choice' (recital 67).

Unlike recitals, 'articles' of an EU law are legally binding. In article 25 of the DSA, deceptive patterns are expressly forbidden:

'Providers of online platforms shall not design, organise or operate their online interfaces in a way that deceives or manipulates the recipients of their service or in a way that otherwise materially distorts or impairs the ability of the recipients of their service to make free and informed decisions.'

Although this provision is rather brief, it immediately goes on to propose that the European Commission may issue further guidelines to expand upon these rules in the future. Specifically:

'The Commission may issue guidelines on how paragraph 1 applies to specific practices, notably: (a) giving more prominence to certain choices when asking the recipient of the service for a decision; (b) repeatedly requesting that the recipient of the service make a choice where that choice has already been made, especially by presenting pop-ups that interfere with the user experience; (c)

making the procedure for terminating a service more difficult than
subscribing to it.'

So, although the DSA only applies to certain kinds of business, and
although the provisions about deceptive patterns are quite brief, the
story isn't over – we can expect more rules to come.

The DSA also contains some important provisions about risk assessments, audits and risk mitigation that will have a significant effect in
the fight against deceptive patterns. These provisions only apply to
VLOPs and VLOSEs – the giants like Amazon and Google. On the one
hand, the fact that these provisions are limited to giants is quite practical: giant businesses have a big impact on EU citizens, and they're
profitable enough to afford the regulatory burden of the extra work.
But on the other hand, smaller entities get to circumvent these stringent requirements and can potentially get away with employing
deceptive patterns. This underlines the challenge regulators face in
ensuring comprehensive oversight and enforcement of rules meant to
prevent deceptive design across all platforms, regardless of size. Here
are some of the relevant provisions in the DSA:

- **Annual risk assessments are required, including assessment
  of deceptive patterns** (article 34): The DSA requires VLOPs
  and VLOSEs to carry out risk assessments to work out what
  areas of their products are likely to break the rules of the DSA.
  The DSA includes rules about deceptive patterns, so this
  means they'll have to investigate their own products and
  create documents explaining where there's risk or presence of
  deceptive patterns. This will also shift some of the cost of
  investigation from the regulator to the business.
- **Risk assessment documentation must be provided to the
  authorities** (article 34): All the supporting documents from the
  risk assessments have to be preserved for at least three years
  and given to the relevant authorities upon request. These
  documents will be a goldmine for regulatory investigators and
  enforcement officers.

- **External experts must carry out independent audits** (article 37): In addition to the annual risk assessments, the business has to engage, at its own expense, an independent, external organisation to carry out audits to ensure compliance with the DSA. These audits will include content about deceptive patterns and recommendations on how to get rid of them. The auditor must be given cooperation, assistance and given full access to internal data by the business.

- **Audit reports will be made publicly available** (article 42): Audit reports are given directly to the authorities, then made available to the general public (though the public version may have commercially sensitive materials redacted). These independent audits are likely to be more objective and comprehensive than internal risk assessments.

- **Negative findings in the audit report must be actioned** (article 37): Within one month of receiving recommendations in the audit report, the business has to adopt an implementation report that explains how they will make changes to comply with the DSA. This means that the independent auditors will play an important role in stamping out deceptive patterns.

- **Enforced by the member state or the European Commission** (article 49): The DSA defines a new body, called a Digital Services Coordinator, which each member state in the EU will have to designate. The coordinator is responsible for all matters relating to the DSA in the member state. However, enforcement of the DSA can be carried out either at a state level or by the European Commission. This will prevent member states from using lax enforcement to entice VLOPs and VLOSEs to base their headquarters locally. If any member state is lax, the European Commission can step in.

In summary, the DSA's risk assessment, audit and risk mitigation provisions are a really big deal in the fight against deceptive patterns – they force businesses and auditors to show when they're using deceptive patterns, and where they might use them in the future. However, this is limited to just VLOPs and VLOSEs, so if a business squeaks in under the size criteria, they don't have to do the risk assessments and audits described above.

All considered, the DSA is a new and exciting addition to EU platform regulation. The DSA packs a hard punch, too: up to 6% of global turnover, risk mitigation measures, and even a ban from the EU in the case of repeated serious breaches.

THE PROPOSED DATA ACT

The Data Act was proposed in February 2022. If approved, it will apply to data sharing and data portability activities. It builds on the GDPR, providing more specific guidance for data sharing and portability. The Data Act aims to enable more data access and reuse among different actors, fostering innovation, competition, and the public interest. Although the Data Act does not introduce a new definition or test for deceptive patterns, it contains provisions that forbid certain kinds of deceptive patterns. For example:

- **Obstructing users from exercising their data protection rights**: A product cannot make it difficult for users to delete their accounts or transfer their data to another service provider by hiding the options in complex menus or requiring multiple steps to complete these actions.
- **False consent in sharing data with a third party**: Any third party that receives data cannot coerce, deceive or manipulate the user in any way, by subverting or impairing the autonomy, decision-making or choices of the user, including by means of a digital interface with the user.

In summary, if it's adopted the Data Act will be a win for users because it will prevent companies from locking in their data and holding it hostage, and instead allow users to take their data to use with a competitor. It also forbids the use of deceptive patterns to try to get around this (and various other data related rules).

THE UCPD GUIDANCE NOTICE

Another notable piece of progress in the European Union is the recent Unfair Commercial Practices Directive guidance notice, which was published by the European Commission in December 2021.[5] These sorts of guidance notices are not legally binding, but they effectively provide an instruction manual to the member states, explaining how to implement and use the directive. What's remarkable about the guidance notice is that it has a section on 'data driven practices and dark patterns' (section 4.2.7), that forbids them. To quote:

'If dark patterns are applied in the context of business-to-consumer commercial relationships, then the Directive can be used to challenge the fairness of such practices. [...] any manipulative practice that materially distorts or is likely to distort the economic behaviour of an average or vulnerable consumer could breach the trader's professional diligence requirements (article 5), amount to a misleading practice (articles 6–7) or an aggressive practice (articles 8–9), depending on the specific dark pattern applied.'

The guidance notice goes on to list numerous specific deceptive patterns that are forbidden under the UCPD:

- **Visual interference**: 'visually obscuring important information or ordering it in a way to promote a specific option'.
- **Obstruction**: 'e.g. one path very long, another shorter'.
- **Trick wording**: 'ambiguous language (e.g. double negatives) to confuse the consumer'.
- **Sneaking**: 'Default interface settings [...] for example by using pre-ticked boxes, including to charge for additional services'.

Since the wheels of commercial law turn slowly, it's quite possible that we haven't yet seen the full impact of this guidance from the European Commission.

If we look at the UCPD guidance together with the DMA, the DSA and proposed Data Act, it's quite obvious which way things are going. Deceptive patterns are a matter of focus for legislation in the EU, and we're likely to see a lot of enforcement action in the coming years, followed by the tech industry waking up to the fact that they need to change their design practices.

CHAPTER 31
CHANGES AFOOT IN THE UNITED STATES

To begin with, it's worth mentioning that the US is not insulated from the EU. For example, the GDPR and DSA have an extraterritorial effect. This means any business in the US has to change their practices in line with European legislation if directing products at Europeans.

EU laws have similar goals and values to the US, so they don't require businesses to do completely opposite things. At present, the EU laws are generally more strict – so if a business complies with EU law, they're also likely to comply with their local US federal and state law at the same time. In theory this should be attractive to US businesses as it will make them less of a target to the increasingly vigilant FTC and the ever-growing class action lawsuit industry.

While the EU has been focusing on legislation, the US has mainly been focusing on enforcement, particularly with a view to preventing anti-competitive behaviour, as it could lead to negative outcomes for the national economy and the wellbeing of its citizens. In July 2021, President Biden signed an executive order that encouraged federal agencies to increase competition and to limit corporate dominance. Around the same time, the president appointed Lina Kahn to be chair of the Federal Trade Commission, an expert in the regulation of anti-competitive behaviour, and passionate about the regulation of deceptive patterns.[1] In a recent announcement, Khan made the agency's position very clear indeed:[2]

'Protecting the public, and especially children, from online privacy invasions and dark patterns is a top priority for the Commission, and these enforcement actions make clear to businesses that the FTC is cracking down on these unlawful practices.'

— LINA KAHN, FTC CHAIR (DECEMBER 19, 2022)

In recent years, the FTC has been ramping up its enforcement actions against companies that employ deceptive patterns. In September 2022, the FTC published a staff report titled 'Bringing Dark Patterns to Light', detailing its position and providing guidance for businesses, with numerous examples of enforcement actions.[3] In November 2022, the FTC reached a $100 million settlement with Vonage, the internet phone service provider, for using deceptive patterns that prevented customers from cancelling their services.[4] Despite allowing customers to sign up for a free trial easily online, the FTC complaint alleged that Vonage forced customers through a difficult cancellation process on the telephone, containing significant hurdles and adding expensive junk fees when they tried to cancel.

In March 2023, the FTC achieved a record $245 million settlement with Epic Games regarding its use of deceptive patterns in the game Fortnite. According to the complaint, Epic Games designed its payment system in a manner that facilitated accidental purchases. Specifically, once credit card details were entered into the Fortnite system, a player could make in-game purchases with a single button press, without a cardholder consent process or any other additional steps (such as a confirmation step, or re-entering the card CVV number). Epic ignored internal feedback from staff and over one million complaints from customers regarding this problem, instead insisting on a no refunds policy. Following the FTC's investigation, this resulted in the largest ever settlement for a case involving deceptive patterns, requiring Epic to return millions of dollars to users and to redesign their payment experience to prevent accidental purchases and to enable straightforward refunds, among other things.

The tech industry has responded to the FTC's recent activity via a think tank called the Information Technology and Innovation Foundation (ITIF). In 2022, ITIF was financially supported by Adobe, Airbnb, Amazon, Apple, Comcast, Facebook, Google, Microsoft, Uber, Verizon, and many others. They have a long history of representing the interests of the tech industry.

In January 2023, ITIF published an article hitting back at the FTC, arguing that 'dark patterns' is an 'alarmist term' that has been 'popularized by anti-technology activists to spread fear'.[5] In the article, ITIF makes some strange arguments. For example, it states that 'accidental purchases […] are not, on their own, illegal' (while true, this is wilfully missing the point), and that 'Neither of these [FTC] complaints were based on a confusing design of Epic's in-game purchasing interface.' This is in direct contradiction with the FTC, which plainly describes the case in its complaint and associated press release: 'Fortnite's counterintuitive, inconsistent, and confusing button configuration led players to incur unwanted charges based on the press of a single button'.[6]

Although the content of the ITIF article is muddled, the tone is very telling. The FTC's recent work has got the tech industry feeling rattled and defensive. We can assume that the changes afoot in the EU are also a source of concern for them.

CHAPTER 32
AI, HYPERNUDGING AND SYSTEM-LEVEL DECEPTIVE PATTERNS

The sudden explosion of AI tools in 2023 has received a great deal of attention from governments, regulators and tech ethicists. It is understood that AI will make misinformation and disinformation campaigns much easier. Deep fakes,[1] bots,[2] and a tidal wave of fake content are among the concerns.[3] The impact of AI on deceptive patterns is less frequently discussed, but the themes are similar.

For example, AI could be used to assist designers in creating conventional deceptive patterns. In the same way that Midjourney[4] and Dall-E[5] can be used to generate images, there is a new wave of tools that can generate user interfaces from text prompts, such as Uizard Autodesigner[6] and TeleportHQ AI website builder,[7] as you can see in the screenshot below:[8]

Which device are you designing for?

☐ Mobile   ☐ Tablet   ☐ Web

Describe your project in plain English   ✨ Try example

a mobile app for delivering food in space to|

Describe a design style, pick keywords, or both

Modern startup aesthetic in the style of Airbnb but more corporate

Light   Dark   Modern   Artsy   Techy   Young

Corporate   Formal   Elegant   Hand-drawn

Generate my project   Alpha

Screenshot of Ulzard Autodesigner

At the time of writing, this type of tool is fairly basic, but given the rapid acceleration of AI, it's reasonable to assume that it could become widespread soon. AI tools are reliant on training data – Midjourney is trained on millions of images from the web, and ChatGPT is trained on millions of articles. Websites and apps today tend to contain deceptive patterns, so if this new wave of UI generator AI tools are trained on them, they will reproduce variations of the same sorts of deceptive patterns unless special efforts are made to prevent them from doing so.

You can imagine a junior designer giving a fairly innocuous text prompt like, 'Cookie consent dialog that encourages opt-in' and receiving in return a design that contains deceptive patterns. A further consequence of AI automation is that design teams will probably be smaller, so there will be fewer staff to provide critique and push back on deceptive patterns when they're created.

In 2003, Swedish philosopher Nick Bostrom conceived a thought experiment called the 'paperclip maximiser'. The idea is that if you give an AI autonomy and a goal to maximise something, you can end up with tragic consequences. In Bostrom's words:[9]

'Suppose we have an AI whose only goal is to make as many paper clips as possible. The AI will realize quickly that it would be much better if there were no humans because humans might decide to switch it off. Because if humans do so, there would be fewer paper clips. Also, human bodies contain a lot of atoms that could be made into paper clips. The future that the AI would be trying to gear towards would be one in which there were a lot of paper clips but no humans.'

– NICK BOSTROM (2003)

Of course, this idea is currently science fiction, but if we swap the idea of a paperclip with *pay per click* – or indeed any kind of design optimisation based on tracked user behaviour – then it suddenly becomes a lot more realistic.

Some aspects of this idea have been around for years. For example, Facebook[10] and Google[11] give business owners the means to load a range of ad variations for A/B testing (measuring click-through rate or similar) and then to have the tool carry out *automatic selection of the winner*. This takes the human out of the loop, so the advertiser can press the 'run' button and then leave it to do the job. If they happen to check in after a few weeks, they'll find that 'survival of the fittest' has occurred. The ads that people didn't click have been killed off, and the ad that was most persuasive at getting clicks has become the winner, shown to all users.

These systems are not autonomous, thankfully: a human has to set it up, provide the design variations and it's limited to just advertisements. With the new generation of AI tools, we can imagine this working at a grander scale, so a human would be able to give a broad, open-ended brief, press 'go' and leave it running forever – writing its own copy, designing and publishing its own pages, crafting its own algorithms, running endless variations and making optimisation improvements based on what it has learned. If the AI tool has no ethical guide rails or concepts of legal compliance, deceptive patterns are inevitable – after all, they're common, easy to build, and generally deliver more clicks than their honest counterparts.

Related to this is the idea of persuasion profiling[12] or hypernudging[13] – a system that tacitly collects behavioural data about what persuasive techniques work on an individual or market segment, and then uses that knowledge to show deceptive patterns that are personally tailored to them. For example, if a system has worked out that you're more susceptible to time pressure than other cognitive biases, it will show you more deceptive patterns that take advantage of time pressure. Research so far has focused on cognitive biases, but it's easy to imagine it being extended to target other types of vulnerability; if the system works out you have dyslexia, it could target your weakness by employing more trick wording in getting you to complete a valuable action like signing a contract. If you have dyscalculia (difficulty with numbers and mental arithmetic) then it could target your weakness by using mathematically tricky combinations of offers, bundles and durations.

In his book *Persuasion Profiling: How the Internet Knows What Makes You Tick*[14], Dr Maurits Kaptein argues that 'Persuasion profiles are the next step in increasing the impact of online marketing' and are 'especially useful if you are trying to sell things online'. The figure below shows a persuasion profile from one of Kaptein's research papers. Each row depicts a 'persuasion principle' derived from Cialdini's 'weapons of influence'.[15] The *x* axis depicts whether the item will have a positive or negative effect in influencing the user's choice.[16]

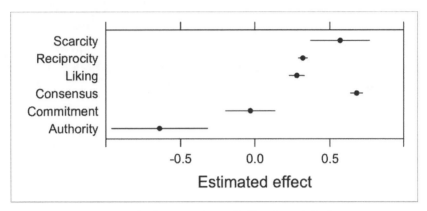

An example of a persuasion profile (Kaptein et al. 2015)

In one research study, Kaptein et al. had hundreds of participants complete a 'susceptibility to persuasion scale' (STPS), deriving persuasion profiles for each individual. They then had the participants carry out a dieting activity in which they were encouraged to eat fewer snacks between meals. They were prompted to log their snacking behaviour via SMS. Unbeknown to them, the prompt SMS messages contained persuasive content that was varied by experimental condition. Those participants who received messages based on their persuasion profile were persuaded more effectively than any other group – they snacked less between meals.

The concept of persuasion profiling is related to so-called psychological warfare tools and the Cambridge Analytica Brexit scandal, in which personalised political messages were covertly sent to individuals in the UK based on illegally acquired personal profiles, thereby influencing the result of the Brexit referendum.[17] It seems this scandal may still be fresh in the minds of EU legislators given the enormous focus on privacy and consumer protection in legislation in recent years.

In a 2023 research paper subtitled 'Manipulation beneath the Interface', legal scholars Mark Leiser and Cristiana Santos put forward the concept of a spectrum of visibility of deceptive patterns.[18] In other words, deceptive patterns range from those that are easily detected by an investigator, to those that are hard to detect without extensive work. Leiser and Santos summarise this spectrum of visibility into three tiers – 'visible', 'darker' and 'darkest', which can be unpacked and described as follows:

- **Self-evident deceptive patterns**: Things like confirmshaming, forced action and nagging are visible for anyone to see. They're brash and rather unmissable.
- **Hidden but UI-based deceptive patterns**: Things like sneaking and misdirection are designed to be insidious and to slip by without the user noticing, but they can be detected by an investigator doing a careful analysis of the pages (that is, they are observable on the pages, which can be screenshotted and highlighted).
- **Multistep business logic deceptive patterns**: This type is algorithmic, but using relatively trivial logic. Imagine a multistep questionnaire where the user answers some questions, and branching logic drives them to one offer or another based on their responses. This sort of deceptive pattern can be investigated by running through the steps multiple times, and representing the behaviour as a flow chart.
- **Complex algorithm-based deceptive patterns**: Traditional personalisation and recommendation systems fall into this category. These algorithms involve complex code and mathematics, and the exact system behaviour cannot accurately be discerned without viewing the system source code (which is typically not available to the public). However, the behaviour is deterministic – given the same inputs, the same result is always given. This means a business can always account for the precise behaviour of their system, though the explanation would most likely involve mathematical formulae or pseudocode.
- **AI-based deceptive patterns**: Systems that learn from user input and employ AI (such as large language models like GPT)

can be inscrutable closed boxes, even to the people who create them. The behaviour of the system is emergent and probability-based. This means that given the same inputs, the system can give different answers to different users or at different points in time. This poses a regulatory challenge because businesses will struggle to account for exactly how their system behaves towards users.

To date, most work on deceptive patterns has been focused on the uppermost visible layers, and there is much more work to be done to understand the deeper, less visible deceptive patterns.

CHAPTER 33
THE RISK OF A TECHNO-DYSTOPIAN FUTURE

Today, many aspects of our lives remain offline. If you walk into a store with nothing but a handful of coins, you know you'll usually be treated just as fairly as the next customer. If you leave your technology at home and go for a hike on a nature trail, you know you're anonymous, untracked and free to commune with nature, uninterrupted. But we're already getting glimpses of a future where that isn't true – where you're perpetually monitored, sold to, manipulated and given a different deal to the next person, owing to some opaque business decision that occurred on a server farm on a different continent. In the 2014 research paper 'Dark Patterns in Proxemic Interactions', Greenberg et al. describe the possibility of science fiction like *Minority Report* or *Black Mirror* happening in real life, where invasive tracking and targeted advertisements can never be avoided.[1] They mention the example of experimental vending machines in Japan that have dynamic pricing based on face recognition, emotion detection, time of day and temperature – in other words, the price is only presented to you once the system has worked out the most you're likely to be willing to pay.[2] In the book *You've Been Played*, Adrian Hon describes the slide of tech industry philosophy into everyday life: how Amazon warehouse workers are tracked and pressured to maximise their physical performance; how Uber drivers are sent personalised 'quests' to keep them driving; and how China scores its citizens to ensure compliant behaviour.[3]

There's something very unsettling about the online world becoming the *only world*, and having no ability to escape it. Perhaps the problem with deceptive pattern research today is not that it's alarmist – as industry lobby group ITIF claims – but actually that it's not alarmist enough?[4]

CHAPTER 34
CONCLUDING THOUGHTS

Perhaps you've read this entire book and you've come to the conclusion, 'Yeah, but I wouldn't do any of that stuff. I'm honest. I'll always respect users and never manipulate or deceive them.'

If you're a designer, a business stakeholder, or any kind of product decision-maker, this is a dangerous way of thinking. It deters you from deeply considering the consequences of product design, particularly in situations where you're under pressure to deliver results.

Instead, I think it's useful to *always think of UI design as an act of persuasion.* If the user's needs and the consequences of your work are not fully considered, then your efforts to persuade are liable to start down a slippery slope and become manipulation or deception. Design is a balancing act between business objectives and user needs. Even seemingly neutral decisions have consequences – if you present one feature prominently in your product, you present other features less prominently as a result. Sometimes these trade-offs are not as harmless as they initially may seem.

I'm reminded of the horror movie cliché where one of the characters explains, to great dramatic effect, that the evil thing pursuing them doesn't feel compassion, can't be reasoned with, and will never stop – whether it's a Terminator, a shark, or some guy in a hockey mask. It's quite a good technique to get the audience on the edge of their seats for the rest of the movie. But here's the thing: software is quite similar. Software is very good at following the same instructions over and over again, it doesn't feel compassion, and it's generally very bad at reflecting on the implications of its actions on the wider world.

Once a user interface has been programmed to behave in a certain way, it will continue to do this with every single human it comes in contact with, whether it's a thousand people a day, a million, or more. The scale is almost unlimited, so the impact of every tiny design decision is magnified and should be considered accordingly.

If you give a human an unkind script to follow in a customer services or sales role, they'll become aware of the implications. In a team, some of them will eventually deviate from the script, apply a little compassion, complain to management, or just leave the job. Unless it's explicitly programmed to, software will never choose to help, or be kind, or go the extra mile for a vulnerable user. Software creates a barrier between the people inside a business and the users outside. Users become anonymous numbers in a spreadsheet, or pixels on a line graph that business stakeholders are trying to move upwards and to the right. Humanity is stripped out and that makes it much easier to do unfair and harmful things through deception and manipulation.

It's worth thinking about the words of Nobel Prize winner Richard Thaler here: 'Whenever anyone asks me to sign a copy of the book *Nudge* I sign it "nudge for good", which is a plea, not an expectation, because it is possible for actors in both the public and private sector to nudge for evil.'[1]

Let's work together to make nudging for good the norm, not the exception. There should be no room for manipulation and deception in our products and markets.

EPILOGUE

The topic of deceptive patterns has evolved rapidly, and it now sits at the intersection between applied psychology, design and law. The next wave of progress needs to incorporate expertise from all three worlds. We need to work together.

In an effort towards this goal, the *deceptive.design* website is now a collaborative project. Dr Mark Leiser, Dr Cristiana Santos and Kosha Doshi have joined the *deceptive.design* team, bringing expertise in legislation and regulation.[1]

The new website joins the dots between deceptive patterns, laws and enforcement. The idea is that when someone reads about a deceptive pattern, they'll be able to also see the laws that pattern breaks in the US or EU, and any legal cases or enforcement actions that have happened, including the size of the fines and the outcomes. The intention is to equip designers, engineers and other employees with new, more powerful materials in the fight against deceptive patterns in their workplace. Instead of going to their boss and saying, 'This is a deceptive pattern. We shouldn't use it or we'll be named and shamed', they will now be able to say 'This is a deceptive pattern. It breaks these specific laws, and these are all the legal cases that have happened to companies that have done this. Look at the size of the penalties they faced.' This is a much more powerful way to talk to business owners – the language of risk and balance sheets.

For us to sustain this project, we need your help. If you see any examples for the hall of shame, share them on social media or send them in using the share section on the site. If you're a researcher who has published something, send us your links for the reading list. And if you're familiar with laws and legal cases, tell us about them. Every contribution, no matter how small, will make a difference.

ABOUT THE AUTHOR

Since 2010, Harry Brignull has dedicated his career to understanding and exposing the manipulative and deceptive techniques that are employed to exploit users online. He is credited with coining a number of the terms that are now popularly used in this research area, and is the founder of the website *deceptive.design* (formerly *darkpatterns.org*). He has worked as an expert witness on a number of cases about deceptive patterns, including Nichols v. Noom Inc. (case 1:20-cv-03677), Arena v. Intuit Inc. (Case 3:19-cv-02546) and FTC v. Publishers Clearing House LLC (Case 2:23-cv-04735). Harry is also an accomplished user experience practitioner, having worked for organisations that include Smart Pension, Spotify, Pearson, HMRC, and the Telegraph newspaper.

ENDNOTES

PROLOGUE

1. C-SPAN. (2021, March 25). House Hearing on Combating Online Misinformation and Disinformation [Video]. C-SPAN. https://www.c-span.org/video/?510053-1/house-hearing-combating-online-misinformation-disinformation&live=#

I. DIVING INTO THE WORLD OF DECEPTION

1. Under advice from the Tech Policy Design Lab of the World Wide Web Foundation, I have stopped using the term 'dark pattern' and now use 'deceptive pattern'. The change reflects a commitment to avoiding language that might inadvertently carry racist associations. In this book, the term 'dark pattern' is used only when referring to laws, quotations and research papers that use the term.
2. This book is not a legal textbook. When the word 'deceptive' is used in this book, it is not intended to confer any sort of legal category or judgement. Please consider it to be intended as a like-for-like replacement of the legacy term 'dark pattern'. In this book, the term 'deceptive pattern' is generally intended as a shorthand for the term 'deceptive or manipulative pattern'.
3. Brignull, H. (2010, October 3). Dark patterns. Retrieved 3 May 2023 from https://old.deceptive.design/ A historical snapshot of darkpatterns.org, which was recently renamed to deceptive.design
4. Flights and airline FAQs | Gatwick Airport. (n.d.). https://www.gatwickairport.com/faqs/flights-and-airlines/
5. Santos, D. (2018, October 9). Customer Paths and Retail Store Layout — Part 3. Aislelabs. https://www.aislelabs.com/blog/2018/09/26/customer-paths-and-retail-store-layout-part-3
6. Image source for figure: Gatwick Airport South Terminal Passenger Maps. (2019, December). Retrieved 3 May 2023 from https://www.gatwickairport.com/globalassets/passenger-facilities/airport-maps/dec-2019/gatwick-airport-south-terminal-passenger-maps---dec-2019.pdf
7. Gatwick key facts | Gatwick Airport. (n.d.). https://www.gatwickairport.com/business-community/about-gatwick/company-information/gatwick-key-facts/
8. Image source for figure: Brignull, H. (2010, September 28). Trick questions - dark patterns. From https://old.deceptive.design/trick_questions/ A historical snapshot of darkpatterns.org.
9. Article 4 of GDPR states '"consent" of the data subject means any freely given, specific, informed and unambiguous indication of the data subject's wishes by which he or she, by a statement or by a clear affirmative action, signifies agreement to the processing of personal data relating to him or her.'
10. European Parliament and Council. (2016, May 27). Regulation (EU) 2016/679. EUR-Lex. Retrieved 5 August 2022 from https://eur-lex.europa.eu/eli/reg/2016/679/oj.

11. Alexander, C., Ishikawa, S., & Silverstein, M. (1977). A pattern language: towns, buildings, construction. New York: Oxford University Press.

12. Regulation (EU) 2022/1925 of the European Parliament and of the Council of 14 September 2022 on contestable and fair markets in the digital sector and amending Directives (EU) 2019/1937 and (EU) 2020/1828 (Digital Markets Act) (Text with EEA relevance). (2022, October 12). EUR-Lex. Retrieved 5 March 2023 from https://eur-lex.europa.eu/eli/reg/2022/1925.

13. Regulation (EU) 2022/2065 of the European Parliament and of the Council of 19 October 2022 on a Single Market For Digital Services and amending Directive 2000/31/EC (Digital Services Act) (Text with EEA relevance). (2022, October 27). EUR-Lex. Retrieved 5 March 2023 from https://eur-lex.europa.eu/eli/reg/2022/2065.

14. Proposal for a Regulation of the European Parliament and of the Council on Harmonised Rules on Fair Access to and Use of Data (Data Act). (2022, February 23). European Commission. https://eur-lex.europa.eu/legal-content/EN/TXT/HTML/?uri=CELEX:52022PC0068

15. The California Consumer Privacy Act of 2018. (2023, January 20). State of California - Department of Justice - Office of the Attorney General. Retrieved 7 February 2023 from https://oag.ca.gov/privacy/ccpa.

16. Colorado Privacy Act. (2021, July 7). https://leg.colorado.gov/sites/default/files/2021a_190_signed.pdf

17. By *enforcer* I mean any entity that acts to ensure compliance with legal regulations and protects consumers from deceptive patterns, either directly or indirectly. Many regulators are enforcers (e.g. the Federal Trade Commission, the Competition and Markets Authority), but enforcement also can occur via private law firms, consumer advocacy groups, and others.

1. A PRIMER ON DESIGN INDUSTRY TERMINOLOGY

1. Competition and Markets Authority. (2022, September 2). Online Choice Architecture: How digital design can harm competition and consumers 2022 (CMA). GOV.UK. Retrieved 2 January 2023 from https://www.gov.uk/find-digital-market-research/online-choice-architecture-how-digital-design-can-harm-competition-and-consumers-2022-cma.

2. r/assholedesign. (n.d.). Reddit. https://www.reddit.com/r/assholedesign/

3. Thaler, R. H., & Sunstein, C. R. (2008). Nudge: Improving decisions about health, wealth, and happiness. Yale University Press.

4. Sunstein, C. R. (2022). Sludge: What stops us from getting things done and what to do about it. MIT Press.

5. A number of the patterns described in this book are not deceptive under the FTC Act's definition of the term *deceptive*, e.g. confirm-shaming, nagging or forced action. Those sorts of patterns are better described as manipulative. Since this book is not a legal text, I have stuck with the term *deceptive patterns* throughout and intend it as a synonym to the term *dark patterns* as used by the FTC and other parties in the US.

2. THE RISE OF DECEPTIVE PATTERNS

1. Stanford Digital Civil Society Lab. (n.d.). Dark Pattern Tipline. Retrieved 3 August 2022 from https://darkpatternstipline.org/
2. Stevens, M. (2016). Cheats and deceits: How animals and plants exploit and mislead. Oxford University Press.
3. Underhill, P. (1999). Why we buy: The science of shopping. Simon & Schuster.
4. JavaScript is a programming language that is typically run in web browsers, allowing websites to be interactive and dynamic.
5. You may also have heard of split testing and multivariate testing (MVT). Both are conceptually similar to A/B testing with some technical differences.
6. Hopkins, Claude C. (1923) Scientific advertising. http://www.scientificadvertising.com/ScientificAdvertising.pdf

3. FROM HOMO ECONOMICUS TO HOMO MANIPULABLE

1. Simon, H. A. (1986). Rationality in psychology and economics. The Journal of Business, 59(4), S209–S224. http://www.jstor.org/stable/2352757
2. Nobel Prize in Economic Sciences 2017: https://www.nobelprize.org/prizes/economic-sciences/2017/press-release/
3. Thaler, R. H., & Sunstein, C. R. (2008). Nudge: Improving decisions about health, wealth, and happiness. Yale University Press.
4. Wickens, C.D., Gordon, S., & Liu, Y. (1997) An introduction to human factors engineering. Longman. https://openlibrary.org/works/OL2728752W/An_introduction_to_human_factors_engineering
5. Jarovsky, L. (2022, March 1). Dark patterns in personal data collection: Definition, taxonomy and lawfulness. https://papers.ssrn.com/sol3/papers.cfm?abstract_id=4048582

II. EXPLOITATIVE STRATEGIES

1. Gray, C. M., Kou, Y., Battles, B., Hoggatt, J., & Toombs, A. L. (2018). The dark (patterns) side of ux design. Proceedings of the 2018 CHI conference on human factors in computing systems. https://doi.org/10.1145/3173574.3174108

4. EXPLOITING PERCEPTUAL VULNERABILITIES

1. Purves, D. (2001). Neuroscience. Palgrave Macmillan.
2. Gleitman, H., Gross, J., & Reisberg, D. (2011). Psychology. WW Norton & Company.
3. Lime hawk-moth | Cumbria Wildlife Trust. (n.d.). https://www.cumbriawildlifetrust.org.uk/wildlife-explorer/invertebrates/moths/lime-hawk-moth
4. Image source for figure: Sale, B. (2018). Lime hawk-moth (Mimas tiliae). Flickr. https://flickr.com/photos/33398884@N03/40578533840. cc-by-2.0.
5. W3C. (n.d.). G17: Ensuring that a contrast ratio of at least 7:1 exists between text (and images of text) and background behind the text | Techniques for WCAG 2.0.

w3.org. Retrieved 3 August 2022 from https://www.w3.org/TR/WCAG20-TECHS/G17.html#G17-tests

6. WebAIM. (n.d.). WebAIM: Contrast checker. webaim.org. Retrieved 3 August 2022 from https://webaim.org/resources/contrastchecker/

7. Atrash, D. (2022, February 8). Understanding web accessibility standards: ADA, Section 508, and WCAG compliance. Medium. https://bootcamp.uxdesign.cc/understanding-web-accessibility-standards-ada-section-508-and-wcag-compliance-143cfb8b691e

8. Arena v. Intuit Inc. Case No. 19-cv-02546-CRB. (2020, March 12). Casetext. Retrieved June 29, 2023, from https://casetext.com/case/arena-v-intuit-inc

9. Arena v. Intuit Inc. Case No. 19-cv-02546-CRB. (2020, March 12). Casetext. Retrieved June 29, 2023, from https://casetext.com/case/arena-v-intuit-inc

10. When taken to the Ninth Circuit, this decision was actually reversed, which demonstrates some ambiguity in the nature of the case and US law.

11. Nouwens, M., Liccardi, I., Veale, M., Karger, D., & Kagal, L. (2020). Dark patterns after the GDPR: Scraping consent pop-ups and demonstrating their influence. Proceedings of the 2020 CHI conference on human factors in computing systems. https://doi.org/10.1145/3313831.3376321

12. The Behavioural Insights Team. (2014a, April 11). EAST: Four simple ways to apply behavioural insights. BIteam.com, 11th Apr 2014. (Box 2.4, Page 24) Retrieved June 17, 2023, from http://www.bi.team/wp-content/uploads/2015/07/BIT-Publication-EAST_FA_WEB.pdf

13. Image source for figure (Note this is from a subsequent, similar study in Louisville): How can a letter encourage us to pay our parking fines? (4 March 2016). The Behavioural Insights Team. Retrieved 17 October 2022 from https://www.bi.team/blogs/how-can-a-letter-encourage-us-to-pay-our-parking-fines/

14. In the plain letter condition, 14.7% of recipients made a payment; while in the red stamp condition, 17.8% of recipients made a payment. The total sample size was 48,445. BIT did not report the numbers assigned to each condition. http://www.bi.team/wp-content/uploads/2015/07/BIT-Publication-EAST_-FA_WEB.pdf

15. Williams, R. (2015). The non-designer's design book: Design and typographic principles for the visual novice. Amsterdam University Press.

5. EXPLOITING VULNERABILITIES IN COMPREHENSION

1. PIAAC: What the Data Say About the Skills of U.S. Adults" (n.d.). Retrieved January 24, 2023, from https://static1.squarespace.com/static/51bb74b8e4b0139570ddf020/t/536a7917e4b058f6a3b2c6cf/1399486743068/PIAAC+Results+Summary_ver508_050614.pdf

2. Infographics. (n.d.). PIAAC Gateway. Retrieved 24 January 2023 from https://www.piaacgateway.com/infographics

3. Image source for figure: Justin Hurwitz, Americans at risk: Manipulation and deception in the digital age. (Written testimony of Justin Hurwitz) (2020) https://www.congress.gov/event/116th-congress/house-event/LC67008/text?loclr=cga-committee

4. Krug, S. (2006). Don't make me think! A common sense approach to web usability. New Riders.

5. This applies to websites and apps in which the user's goals are at odds with the volume of content ('I want to find a way to quickly get through this content so I complete my task'). The obvious exception here is novels and long-form content, when the user's goal is to study or enjoy every single word, despite the high cost of doing so in time, attention and energy.
6. Morkes, J., & Nielsen, J. (1997, January 1) Concise, SCANNABLE, and objective: How to write for the web https://www.nngroup.com/articles/concise-scannable-and-objective-how-to-write-for-the-web/
7. Nielsen, J. (1997, September 30). How users read on the web https://www.nngroup.com/articles/how-users-read-on-the-web/
8. Pernice, K., Whitenton, K.. & Nielsen, J. (2014). How people read online: The eyetracking evidence https://www.nngroup.com/reports/how-people-read-web-eyetracking-evidence/
9. Pirolli, P., & Card, S.K. (1999). Information foraging. Psychological Review, 106(4), 643–675. https://doi.org/10.1037/0033-295X.106.4.643
10. Federal Trade Commission. (2022, September 15). Bringing dark patterns to light - FTC staff report. Retrieved 1 January 2023 from https://www.ftc.gov/reports/bringing-dark-patterns-light
11. Luguri, J., & Strahilevitz, L.J. (2021, January 1). Shining a light on dark patterns. Journal of Legal Analysis, 13(1), 43–109. https://academic.oup.com/jla/article/13/1/43/6180579

6. EXPLOITING VULNERABILITIES IN DECISION-MAKING

1. Society for Judgment and Decision Making. (n.d.). Retrieved 23 January 2023 from https://sjdm.org/
2. Wylie, C. (2020). Mindf*ck: Cambridge Analytica and the plot to break America. Penguin Random House.
3. Ariely, D. (2010). Predictably irrational: The hidden forces that shape our decisions. Revised and expanded edition. Harper Perennial.
4. Sloman, A. (1989). Preface. In M. Sharples, D. Hogg, S. Torrance, D. Young, & C. Hutchinson, Computers and thought: A practical introduction to artificial intelligence. Bradford Books. https://www.cs.bham.ac.uk/research/projects/cogaff/personal-ai-sloman-1988.html
5. Benson, B. (2016, September 1). Cognitive bias cheat sheet: An organized list of cognitive biases because thinking is hard. Better Humans. Medium. Retrieved 23 September 2022 from https://betterhumans.pub/cognitive-bias-cheat-sheet-55a472476b18
6. Cialdini, R.B. (2001). Influence: Science and practice. Allyn and Bacon. The book details '7 weapons of influence': scarcity, authority, social proof, sympathy, reciprocity, consistency and unity.
7. Schüll, N.D. (2014). Addiction by design: Machine gambling in Las Vegas. Amsterdam University Press.
8. 250 best A/B testing ideas based on neuromarketing. (n.d.). Convertize.com. Retrieved 31 January 2023 from https://tactics.convertize.com/principles
9. Johnson, E., & Goldstein, D. A. (2003). Do defaults save lives? Science, 302(5649), 1338–1339. https://doi.org/10.1126/science.1091721
10. Thaler, R.H. (2015). Misbehaving: The making of behavioural economics. Penguin Books Ltd.

11. Servicio Nacional del Consumidor [SERNAC]. (2022, March). Policy paper on cookies consent requests: Experimental evidence of privacy by default and dark patterns on consumer privacy decision making. Retrieved 28 January 2023 from https://icpen.org/sites/default/files/2022-05/SERNAC_Policy_Paper_Cookies_-Experiment.pdf

12. Tversky, A., & Kahneman, D. (1974). Judgement under uncertainty: Heuristics and biases. Science, 185, 1124–1131. https://doi.org/10.1126/science.185.4157.1124

13. Tversky, A., & Kahneman, D. (1981). The framing of decisions and the psychology of choice. Science, 211, 453–458. https://doi.org/10.1126/science.7455683

14. Ariely, D. (2010). Predictably irrational: The hidden forces that shape our decisions. Revised and expanded edition. Harper Perennial.

15. Hallsworth, M., List, J.A., Metcalfe, R.D., & Vlaev, I. (2017). The behavioralist as tax collector: Using natural field experiments to enhance tax compliance. Journal of Public Economics, 148, 14–31. https://doi.org/10.1016/j.jpubeco.2017.02.003

16. Ninja Foodi Air Fryer. (n.d.). Amazon.co.uk. Retrieved 4 February 2023 from https://www.amazon.co.uk/Ninja-Foodi-Fryer-Dual-Zone/dp/B08CN3G4N9/

17. Brignull, H. (2021, May 21). Manipulating app store reviews with dark patterns. 90 Percent of Everything. Retrieved 4 February 2023 from https://90percentofeverything.com/2012/05/21/manipulating-app-store-reviews-with-dark-patterns/

18. Worchel, S., Lee, J. W., & Adewole, A. (1975). Effects of supply and demand on ratings of object value. Journal of Personality and Social Psychology, 32(5), 906–914. https://citeseerx.ist.psu.edu/viewdoc/download?doi=10.1.1.822.9487

19. Arkes, H.R., & Blumer, C. (1985). The psychology of sunk cost. Organizational Behavior and Human Decision Processes, 35(1), 124–140. https://doi.org/10.1016/0749-5978(85)90049-4

20. Behavioural Insights Team with Cabinet Office, Department of Health, Driver and Vehicle Licensing Agency, & NHS Blood and Transplant. (2013, December 23). Applying behavioural insights to organ donation. Behavioural Insights Team. Retrieved 17 October 2022 from https://www.bi.team/publications/applying-behavioural-insights-to-organ-donation/

21. For more information on the use of cognitive biases in persuasion, read Cialdini, R.B. (2001). Influence: Science and Practice. Allyn and Bacon. The book details '7 weapons of influence': scarcity, authority, social proof, sympathy, reciprocity, consistency and unity.

7. EXPLOITING EXPECTATIONS

1. Frost, B. (2013). Atomic design. https://atomicdesign.bradfrost.com/

2. Nikolaus, U., & Bohnert, S. (2017, September 28). User expectations vs. web design patterns: User expectations for the location of web objects revisited. Retrieved 22 January 2023 from https://www.hfes-europe.org/wp-content/uploads/2017/10/Nikolaus2017poster.pdf

3. Podestà, S. (2017, June 26). Digital patterns: A marketing perspective. Medium. https://silviapodesta.medium.com/digital-patterns-a-marketing-perspective-4abf1833cc57

4. Forney, J. (2014). Dark patterns: Ethical design as strategy [I694 thesis project report]. Indiana University at Bloomington.

8. RESOURCE DEPLETION AND PRESSURE

1. Whitenton, K. (2013, December 22). Minimize cognitive load to maximize usability. NN Group. https://www.nngroup.com/articles/minimize-cognitive-load/
2. Interactive Design Foundation. (n.d.). Cognitive friction. https://www.interaction-design.org/literature/topics/cognitive-friction
3. Hockey, R. (2013). The psychology of fatigue: Work, effort and control. Cambridge University Press. https://doi.org/10.1017/CBO9781139015394
4. Sunstein, C.R. (2022). Sludge: What stops us from getting things done and what to do about it. MIT Press.
5. Obstruction: https://www.deceptive.design/types/obstruction
6. Roach motel: https://old.deceptive.design/roach_motel/
7. Specifically: 19.2% of 3,215 people in the extra-step group; versus 24.3% of 5,215 people in the direct group.

9. FORCING AND BLOCKING

1. Defeat Keurig's K-Cup DRM with a single piece of tape. (2014, December 11). [Video]. Boing Boing. Retrieved 12 March 2023 from https://boingboing.net/2014/12/11/defeat-keurigs-k-cup-drm-wit.html
2. Harding, S. (2023, March 9). HP outrages printer users with firmware update suddenly bricking third-party ink. Ars Technica. https://arstechnica.com/gadgets/2023/03/customers-fume-as-hp-blocks-third-party-ink-from-more-of-its-printers/

10. EXPLOITING EMOTIONAL VULNERABILITIES

1. Krishen, A.S., & Bui, M. (2015). Fear advertisements: Influencing consumers to make better health decisions. International Journal of Advertising, 34(3), 533–548. https://doi.org/10.1080/02650487.2014.996278
2. The pair of advertisements in this figure employ sexist imagery and offensive content. While these tactics are objectionable and in poor taste, they illustrate the topic of this chapter—'exploitation of emotional vulnerabilities'.
3. Chapman, S. (2018). Is it unethical to use fear in public health campaigns? American Journal of Public Health, 108(9), 1120–1122. https://doi.org/10.2105/ajph.2018.304630

11. EXPLOITING ADDICTION

1. American Psychiatric Association. (2022). Diagnostic and statistical manual of mental disorders (5th ed., text rev.). APA Publishing. https://doi.org/10.1176/appi.books.9780890425787
2. Griffiths, M.D. (2005). A 'components' model of addiction within a biopsychosocial framework. Journal of Substance Use, 10(4), 191–197. https://doi.org/10.1080/14659890500114359

3. Mujica, A.D., Crowell, C.R., Villano, M., & Uddin, K. (2022). Addiction by design: Some dimensions and challenges of excessive social media use. Medical Research Archives, 10(2). https://esmed.org/MRA/mra/article/view/2677

4. Nestler, E.J. (2005). Is there a common molecular pathway for addiction? Nature Neuroscience, 8(11), 1445–1449. https://doi.org/10.1038/nn1578

5. Pandey, E. (2017, November 9). Sean Parker: Facebook was designed to exploit human 'vulnerability.' Axios. https://www.axios.com/2017/12/15/sean-parker-facebook-was-designed-to-exploit-human-vulnerability-1513306782

6. Skinner, B.F. (1938). The behavior of organisms: An experimental analysis. New York: D. Appleton-Century Company.

7. Mujica, A.D., Crowell, C.R., Villano, M., & Uddin, K. (2022). Addiction by design: Some dimensions and challenges of excessive social media use. Medical Research Archives, 10(2). https://esmed.org/MRA/mra/article/view/2677

8. Eyal, N., & Hoover, R. (2014). Hooked: How to build habit-forming products. Portfolio.

9. Schüll, N.D. (2014). Addiction by design: Machine gambling in Las Vegas. Amsterdam University Press.

10. Knowles, T. (2019, April 27). I'm so sorry, says inventor of endless online scrolling. The Times. Retrieved 28 May 2023 from https://www.thetimes.co.uk/article/i-m-so-sorry-says-inventor-of-endless-online-scrolling-9lrv59mdk

11. Kelly, M. (2019, July 30). New bill would ban autoplay videos and endless scrolling. The Verge. https://www.theverge.com/2019/7/30/20746878/josh-hawley-dark-patterns-platform-design-autoplay-youtube-videos-scrolling-snapstreaks-illegal

12. Forbrukerrådet [Norwegian Consumer Council]. (2022, May 31). Insert coin: How the gaming industry exploits consumers using loot boxes. Retrieved May 19, 2023, from https://fil.forbrukerradet.no/wp-content/uploads/2022/05/2022-05-31-insert-coin-publish.pdf
    Also see: Gambling Commission. (2018, September 17). International concern over blurred lines between gambling and video games. Gambling Commission. https://www.gamblingcommission.gov.uk/news/article/international-concern-over-blurred-lines-between-gambling-and-video-games

13. Macey, J., & Hamari, J. (2022). Gamblification: A definition. New Media & Society. https://doi.org/10.1177/14614448221083903

14. Riendeau, D. (2017, October 20). We talk EA woes, Mass Effect: Andromeda, race, and sexism with Manveer Heir. Waypoint Radio. https://www.vice.com/en/article/evbdzm/race-in-games-ea-woes-with-former-mass-effect-manveer-heir

15. Apple Inc. (2017). App Store review guidelines - Apple Developer. Apple Developer. https://developer.apple.com/app-store/review/guidelines/#in-app-purchase

16. Robertson, A. (2019, May 29). Google's Play Store starts requiring games with loot boxes to disclose their odds. The Verge. https://www.theverge.com/2019/5/29/18644648/google-play-store-loot-box-disclosure-family-friendly-policy-changes

17. Rousseau, J. (2022, August 4). Study finds that Belgium's loot box ban isn't being enforced. GamesIndustry.biz. https://www.gamesindustry.biz/study-finds-that-belgiums-loot-box-ban-isnt-being-enforced

18. Wawro, A. (2017, November 7). Take-Two plans to only release games with 'recurrent consumer spending' hooks. Game Developer. https://www.gamedeveloper.com/business/take-two-plans-to-only-release-games-with-recurrent-consumer-spending-hooks

19. DarkPattern.games. Healthy gaming: Avoid addictive gaming dark patterns. (n.d.). DarkPattern.games. Retrieved 19 May 2023 from https://www.darkpattern.games/
20. Forbrukerrådet [Norwegian Consumer Council]. (2022, May 31). Insert coin: How the gaming industry exploits consumers using loot boxes. Retrieved 19 May 2023 from https://fil.forbrukerradet.no/wp-content/uploads/2022/05/2022-05-31-insert-coin-publish.pdf
21. Goodstein, S. (2021, February 1). When the cat's away: Techlash, loot boxes, and regulating 'dark patterns' in the video game industry's monetization strategies. University of Colorado Law Review. Retrieved 19 May 2023 from https://lawreview.colorado.edu/printed/when-the-cats-away-techlash-loot-boxes-and-regulating-dark-patterns-in-the-video-game-industrys-monetization-strategies/

12. DRAWING A LINE BETWEEN PERSUASION AND MANIPULATION

1. Although I use the term 'deceptive pattern' throughout this book, I actually use the term 'deceptive or manipulative patterns' when I'm working in legal contexts.
2. Sunstein, C.R. (2015, February 18). Fifty Shades of Manipulation. Social Science Research Network. https://doi.org/10.2139/ssrn.2565892

III. TYPES OF DECEPTIVE PATTERN

1. Gray, C. M., Kou, Y., Battles, B., Hoggatt, J., & Toombs, A. L. (2018). The dark (patterns) side of ux design. Proceedings of the 2018 CHI conference on human factors in computing systems. https://doi.org/10.1145/3173574.3174108
2. EDPB. (2022, March 14). Dark patterns in social media platform interfaces: How to recognise and avoid them. European Data Protection Board. Retrieved 14 January 2023 from https://edpb.europa.eu/system/files/2022-03/edpb_03-2022_guidelines_on_dark_patterns_in_social_media_platform_interfaces_en.pdf
3. Dark commercial patterns. (2022). OECD Digital Economy Papers. https://doi.org/10.1787/44f5e846-en
4. Mathur, A., Kshirsagar, M., & Mayer, J. (2021). What makes a dark pattern... dark? Proceedings of the 2021 CHI conference on human factors in computing systems. https://doi.org/10.1145/3411764.3445610

13. INTRODUCING THE MATHUR ET AL. TAXONOMY

1. Mathur, A., Acar, G., Friedman, M.J., Lucherini, E., Mayer, J., Chetty, M., and Narayanan, A. (2019). Dark patterns at scale: Findings from a crawl of 11K shopping websites. Proceedings of the ACM on human–computer interaction, 3(CSCW), article 81. https://doi.org/10.1145/3359183
2. Brignull, H. (2013, August 29). Dark patterns: Inside the interfaces designed to trick you. The Verge. https://www.theverge.com/2013/8/29/4640308/dark-patterns-inside-the-interfaces-designed-to-trick-you
3. If you're struggling to see this table on an e-reader, you may find the Mathur et al. website more legible: https://webtransparency.cs.princeton.edu/dark-patterns/
4. I've taken a small liberty in the terminology here. I have renamed the Mathur et al. term 'Trick questions' to 'Trick wording', because tricky language isn't always

phrased in the form of a simple question.

14. SNEAKING

1. Nielsen, J. (2006, December 3). Progressive disclosure. Nielsen Norman Group. Retrieved 21 December 2022 from https://www.nngroup.com/articles/progressive-disclosure/

2. Image source for figure: Sports Direct. (n.d.). Retrieved 4 May 2015 from https://sportsdirect.com

3. Image source for figure: Sports Direct. (n.d.). Retrieved 4 May 2015 from https://sportsdirect.com

4. Consumer Rights Directive (2011) https://eur-lex.europa.eu/legal-content/EN/TXT/?uri=celex%3A32011L0083

5. Federal Trade Commission. The economics of drip pricing. (2015, January 6). Retrieved 10 October 2022 from https://www.ftc.gov/news-events/events/2012/05/economics-drip-pricing

6. Bait and switch: A type of deceptive design. (2010). Retrieved 10 October 2022 from https://www.deceptive.design/types/bait-and-switch

7. Blake, T., Moshary, S., Sweeney, K., & Tadelis, S. (2021, July). Price salience and product choice. Marketing Science, 40(4), 619–636. https://doi.org/10.1287/mksc.2020.1261

8. Image source for screengrab: Stubhub.com screenshots taken on 18 September 2022 while purchasing a ticket to see Bill Burr at Wells Fargo Arena, Des Moines, 8 October 2022.

9. Serati, N. (2019, May 16). The ugly side of Marriott's new home rentals: Sky-high cleaning fees. Thrifty Traveler. Retrieved 10 October 2022 from https://thriftytraveler.com/news/hotels/marriott-cleaning-fees-homes-villas/

10. Pennsylvania Office of Attorney General. AG Shapiro's action requires Marriott to disclose 'resort fees.' (n.d.). Retrieved 10 October 2022 from https://www.attorneygeneral.gov/taking-action/ag-shapiros-action-requires-marriott-to-disclose-resort-fees/

11. Image source for figure: alexa. (2021, May 17). we gotta stop airbnb. Twitter. Retrieved 10 October 2022 from https://twitter.com/mariokartdwi/status/1394176793616080896

12. Shon, S. (2021, June 22). Demystifying Airbnb fees: How to understand the final cost before booking. The Points Guy. Retrieved 10 October 2022 from https://thepointsguy.com/guide/understand-airbnb-fees/

13. Sawyer, D. (2017, December 28). I built a browser extension. Reddit. Retrieved 10 October 2022 from https://www.reddit.com/r/Frugal/comments/7mpca2/i_built_a_browser_extension_that_shows_you_the/

14. ACCC. Price displays. (2022, October 6). Australian Competition and Consumer Commission. Retrieved 10 October 2022 from https://www.accc.gov.au/consumers/pricing/price-displays

15. Schaal, D. (2019, July 13). Airbnb offers greater price transparency in Europe after regulatory threats. Skift. Retrieved 10 October 2022 from https://skift.com/2019/07/15/airbnb-offers-greater-price-transparency-in-europe-after-regulatory-threats/

16. Airbnb.co.uk. (n.d.). Airbnb. Retrieved 10 October 2022 from https://www.airbnb.co.uk/

17. Image source for figure: Airbnb.co.uk. (n.d.). Airbnb. Retrieved 10 October 2022 from https://www.airbnb.co.uk/
18. Screenshot in figure captured from the Figma App on 4 July 2023
19. Screenshot for figure captured on 5 December 2022 from: https://help.figma.com/hc/en-us/articles/360040531773-Share-or-embed-your-files-and-prototypes
20. Image source for figure: Weichbrodt, G. (2021, March 9). Hey @figmadesign, could you please tell people that they're being charged extra money if they submit this form. Twitter. Retrieved 8 May 2023 from https://twitter.com/greg00r/status/1369308234318766091
21. Source for screenshot in figure: How to add a base collaborator. Airtable support. (n.d.). https://support.airtable.com/hc/en-us/articles/202625759-Adding-a-base-collaborator
22. harper. (2020, June 15). just got a $3360 charge from @airtable because i invited some folks to review a base i made. Twitter. Retrieved 8 May 2023 from https://twitter.com/harper/status/1272549461391290370

15. URGENCY

1. Twozillas. (n.d.). Hurrify - Countdown timer: Powerful, effective & instant sales booster. Shopify App Store. Retrieved 1 September 2022 from https://web.archive.org/web/20220901000625/https://apps.shopify.com/hurrify-countdown-timer. Page archive hosted by archive.org.
2. Bogle, A. (2018, January 24). Are five people really looking at this item right now? For consumers, it's hard to know. ABC News. https://www.abc.net.au/news/science/2018-01-25/online-shopping-are-five-people-really-looking-at-this-item/9353788
3. Twozillas. (n.d.). Hurrify - Countdown timer: Powerful, effective & instant sales booster. Shopify App Store. Retrieved 1 September 2022 from https://web.archive.org/web/20220901000625/https://apps.shopify.com/hurrify-countdown-timer. Page archive hosted by archive.org.
4. Samsung Electronics America. Jet 75 cordless vacuum (n.d.). Retrieved 21 December 2022 from https://www.samsung.com/us/home-appliances/vacuums/jet-stick/samsung-jet--75-complete-cordless-stick-vacuum-vs20t7551p5-aa/
5. Samsung Electronics America. Jet 75 cordless vacuum (n.d.). Retrieved 1 November 2022 from https://web.archive.org/web/20221101145349/https://www.samsung.com/us/home-appliances/vacuums/jet-stick/samsung-jet--75-complete-cordless-stick-vacuum-vs20t7551p5-aa/
6. Image source for figure: Samsung Electronics Ameria. Jet 75 cordless vacuum (n.d.). Retrieved 1 November 2022 from https://web.archive.org/web/20221101145349/https://www.samsung.com/us/home-appliances/vacuums/jet-stick/samsung-jet--75-complete-cordless-stick-vacuum-vs20t7551p5-aa

16. MISDIRECTION

1. Joseph, E. (1992). How to pick pockets for fun and profit: A magician's guide to pickpocket magic. Adfo Books.

2. confirmshaming. (n.d.). Confirmshaming. Retrieved 3 August 2022 from https://confirmshaming.tumblr.com/

3. If you're particularly eagle-eyed, you'll notice that confirmshaming is probably better described as a *manipulative* pattern rather than deceptive, since there is no information withheld from the user. For the sake of simplicity and a catchy name, I have taken the liberty of using the term 'deceptive patterns' as a shorthand for both manipulative and deceptive. For a detailed analysis of the difference of the two, refer to 'The Ethics of Manipulation' (Stanford Encyclopedia of Philosophy). (2022, April 21). https://plato.stanford.edu/entries/ethics-manipulation/

4. Image source for figure: Alex9zo. (2017, June 22). No thanks, I hate free money. Reddit. Retrieved 3 August 2022 from https://www.reddit.com/r/mildlyinfuriating/comments/6it8q1/no_thanks_i_hate_free_money/

5. Axbom, P. [axbom]. (2021, August 29). Per Axbom [Tweet]. Twitter. https://twitter.com/axbom/status/1432004956190556163

6. Image source for figure: Axbom, P. [axbom]. (2021, August 29). Per Axbom [Tweet]. Twitter. https://twitter.com/axbom/status/1432004956190556163

7. Sunflower, [ohhellohellohii]. (2021, January 27). @darkpatterns this one nearly got me. @trello really wants you to use their free trial [Tweet]. Twitter. https://twitter.com/ohhellohellohii/status/1354535533456879618

8. Image source for figure: Sunflower, [ohhellohellohii]. (2021, January 27). @darkpatterns this one nearly got me. @trello really wants you to use their free trial [Tweet]. Twitter. https://twitter.com/ohhellohellohii/status/1354535533456879618

9. Image source for figure: Sunflower, [ohhellohellohii]. (2021, January 27). @darkpatterns this one nearly got me. @trello really wants you to use their free trial [Tweet]. Twitter. https://twitter.com/ohhellohellohii/status/1354535533456879618

10. Apple. (n.d.). Accessibility - Vision. Apple (United Kingdom). https://www.apple.com/uk/accessibility/vision/

11. Image source for figure: Atlassian. (n.d.). Try Trello Premium free for 30 days. Trello.com. Retrieved 5 November 2021 from https://trello.com/

12. bigslabomeat. (2021, January 20). Getting desperate now? This came up when I opened the @YouTube app. I don't want premium [Tweet]. Twitter. https://twitter.com/bigolslabomeat/status/1351819681619976198

13. Image source for figure: bigslabomeat. (2021, January 20). Getting desperate now? This came up when I opened the @YouTube app. I don't want premium [Tweet]. Twitter. https://twitter.com/bigolslabomeat/status/1351819681619976198

14. At the time of writing, Tesla's self-driving capabilities are only level 2 automation and not 'full' self-driving. This means it's trick wording or false advertising. For more information see Morris, J. (2021, March 13). Why is Tesla's full self-driving only level 2 autonomous? Forbes. https://www.forbes.com/sites/jamesmorris/2021/03/13/why-is-teslas-full-self-driving-only-level-2-autonomous/

15. Ted Stein on Twitter. (2020, January 20). Twitter. Retrieved 8 May 2023 from https://web.archive.org/web/20200120235411/https://twitter.com/tedstein/status/1219406818415456268

16. Image source for figure: Ted Stein on Twitter. (2020, January 20). Twitter. Retrieved 8 May 2023 from https://web.archive.org/web/20200120235411/https://twitter.com/tedstein/status/1219406818415456268

17. Taleb, N.N. (2020, January 15). Elon @elonmusk, your Customer Support at Tesla is even worse than I claimed last time [Tweet]. https://twitter.com/nntaleb/status/1217471369350348807

18. Source of screenshot in figure: https://teslamotorsclub.com/tmc/threads/anyone-here-get-a-refund-for-acceleration-boost.183979/

19. Goldmacher, S. (2021, April 17). G.O.P. group warns of 'defector' list if donors uncheck recurring box. The New York Times. https://www.nytimes.com/2021/04/07/us/politics/republicans-donations-trump-defector.html

20. Source of image in screenshot: Donald J. Trump's digital donation portal. (n.d.). Winred. Retrieved 13 March 2020 from https://web.archive.org/web/20200313042615/https://secure.winred.com/djt/we-made-history?amount=150&location=websitenav

21. Brignull, H. (2015, April 1). Ryanair hide free option: Don't insure me. darkpatterns.org. Retrieved 8 May 2023 from https://web.archive.org/web/20150804081628/http://darkpatterns.org/ryanair-hide-free-option-dont-insure-me/

22. Autorita' Garante della Concorrenza e del Mercato (AGCM). https://en.agcm.it/en/media/press-releases/2014/2/alias-2105 (last visited 17 Jan 2021).

23. Forbrukerrådet [Norwegian Consumer Council]. Regarding deceptive design on your website. (2022, December 1). Retrieved 28 May 2023 from https://storage02.forbrukerradet.no/media/2022/11/brev-ryanair-engelsk.pdf

24. Competition and Markets Authority. (2019, September 13). Online hotel booking. GOV.UK. Retrieved 13 October 2022 from https://www.gov.uk/cma-cases/online-hotel-booking

25. Competition and Markets Authority. (2019, February 26). Consumer protection law compliance: Principles for businesses offering online accommodation booking services. GOV.UK. Retrieved 13 October 2022 from https://bit.ly/436v4l5

26. Cheplyaka, R. (2017, September 23). How Booking.com manipulates you. Roche.info. Retrieved 3 August 2022 from https://ro-che.info/articles/2017-09-17-booking-com-manipulation

27. Competition and Markets Authority. (2019, February 6). Hotel booking sites to make major changes after CMA probe. GOV.UK. Retrieved 13 October 2022 from https://www.gov.uk/government/news/hotel-booking-sites-to-make-major-changes-after-cma-probe

17. SOCIAL PROOF

1. Image source for figure: Neves-Charge, H., [henry_neves7]. (2017, November 29). This sort of stuff needs to stop. It's a lie and a dark pattern. See it on almost every e-commerce site. #ux #badux #darkpattern #usability @Etsy [Tweet]. Retrieved 8 May 2023 from https://twitter.com/henry_neves7/status/935960327312855040

2. Image source for figure: Beeketing and related apps no longer on Shopify: Details and alternative apps. (2022, January 31). Shopify Community. https://community.shopify.com/c/announcements/beeketing-and-related-apps-no-longer-on-shopify-details-and/td-p/553686

3. Image source for figure: Sales Pop. The world's best social proof app (free!). (n.d.). Retrieved 8 October 2022 from https://beeketing.com/powered-by-sales-pop

4. Beeketing. How to create custom notifications with Sales Pop? (2019, February 27). https://support.beeketing.com/support/solutions/articles/6000162593-how-to-create-custom-notifications-with-sales-pop

5. Image source for figure: Beeketing. How to create custom notifications with Sales Pop? (2019, February 27). https://support.beeketing.com/support/solutions/articles/6000162593-how-to-create-custom-notifications-with-sales-pop
6. Federal Trade Commission. (2022, September 15). Bringing dark patterns to light - FTC staff report. Retrieved 1 January 2023 from https://www.ftc.gov/reports/bringing-dark-patterns-light
7. FTC v. RagingBull.com LLC. Case 1:20-cv-03538-GLR https://www.ftc.gov/system/files/documents/cases/ragingbull.com_-_amended_complaint_for_permanent_injunction_and_other_equitable_relief.pdf

18. SCARCITY

1. Image source for figure: HeyMerch. (n.d.). Hey!Scarcity Low Stock Counter. Shopify App Store. Retrieved 21 December 2022 from https://apps.shopify.com/heymerch-sales-stock-counter
2. Shopify. (n.d.). Requirements for apps in the Shopify App Store. Retrieved 21 December 2022 from https://shopify.dev/apps/store/requirements
3. Effective Apps. (n.d.). Scarcity++ Low Stock Counter. Shopify App Store. Retrieved 21 December 2022 from https://apps.shopify.com/almostgone-low-in-stock-alert
4. Image source for figure: Effective Apps. (n.d.). Scarcity++ Low Stock Counter. Shopify App Store. Retrieved 21 December 2022 from https://apps.shopify.com/almostgone-low-in-stock-alert

19. OBSTRUCTION

1. European Parliament and Council. (2016, May 27). Regulation (EU) 2016/679. EUR-Lex. Retrieved 5 August 2022 from https://eur-lex.europa.eu/eli/reg/2016/679/oj
2. Forbrukerrådet [Norwegian Consumer Council]. (2018, June 18). Deceived by design: How tech companies use dark patterns to discourage us from exercising our rights to privacy. Retrieved 8 March 2023 from https://fil.forbrukerradet.no/wp-content/uploads/2018/06/2018-06-27-deceived-by-design-final.pdf
3. Image source for figure: Forbrukerrådet [Norwegian Consumer Council]. (2018, June 18). Deceived by design: How tech companies use dark patterns to discourage us from exercising our rights to privacy. Retrieved 8 March 2023 from https://fil.forbrukerradet.no/wp-content/uploads/2018/06/2018-06-27-deceived-by-design-final.pdf
4. Image source for figure: Forbrukerrådet [Norwegian Consumer Council]. (2018, June 18). Deceived by design: How tech companies use dark patterns to discourage us from exercising our rights to privacy. Retrieved 8 March 2023 from https://fil.forbrukerradet.no/wp-content/uploads/2018/06/2018-06-27-deceived-by-design-final.pdf
5. BEUC. (2022, June 30). European consumer groups take action against Google for pushing users towards its surveillance system. Retrieved 25 May 2023 from https://www.beuc.eu/press-releases/european-consumer-groups-take-action-against-google-pushing-users-towards-its
6. Brignull, H. (2010). Roach Motel - Dark Patterns. Retrieved June 29, 2023, from https://old.deceptive.design/roach_motel/

7. vanillatary. (2021, November 10). this should literally be illegal [tweet]. Twitter. Retrieved 8 May 2023 from https://twitter.com/vanillatary/status/1458489382327967747

8. Image source for figure: vanillatary. (2021, November 10). this should literally be illegal [tweet]. Twitter. Retrieved 8 May 2023 from https://twitter.com/vanillatary/status/1458489382327967747

9. jandll. (2021, February 18). Before buying a NYT subscription, here's what it'll take to cancel it. Hacker News. Retrieved 8 May 2023 from https://news.ycombinator.com/item?id=26174269

10. Business and professions code, article 9, Automatic purchase renewals [17600–17606]. https://leginfo.legislature.ca.gov/faces/codes_displaySection.xhtml?lawCode=BPC&sectionNum=17602.

11. Consider the Consumer. (2021, June 14). Maribel Moses settlement – California New York Times auto subscription class action lawsuit settles for $5 Million.... https://considertheconsumer.com/class-action-settlements/maribel-moses-settlement-california-new-york-times-auto-subscription-class-action-lawsuit-settles-for-5-5-million

12. Top Class Actions. (2021, August 6). Washington Post auto-renew $6.8m class action settlement. https://topclassactions.com/lawsuit-settlements/closed-settlements/1028395-washington-post-auto-renew-6-8m-class-action-settlement/

13. Federal Trade Commission (2020, September 2). Children's online learning program ABCmouse to pay $10 million to settle FTC charges of illegal marketing and billing practices. https://www.ftc.gov/news-events/press-releases/2020/09/childrens-online-learning-program-abcmouse-pay-10-million-settle

14. Forbrukerrådet [Norwegian Consumer Council]. (2021). You can log out, but you can never leave: How Amazon manipulates consumers to keep them subscribed to Amazon Prime. Retrieved 25 May 2023 from https://fil.forbrukerradet.no/wp-content/uploads/2021/01/2021-01-14-you-can-log-out-but-you-can-never-leave-final.pdf

15. European Commission. (2022, July 1). Consumer protection: Amazon Prime changes its cancellation practices to comply with EU consumer rules. Retrieved 25 May 2023 from https://ec.europa.eu/commission/presscorner/detail/en/ip_22_4186

16. Public Citizen. (2021, January 14). FTC complaint: Ending an Amazon Prime membership is a deceptive, unlawful ordeal. https://www.citizen.org/news/ftc-complaint-ending-an-amazon-prime-membership-is-a-deceptive-unlawful-ordeal/

17. Kim, E. (2022, March 14). Internal documents show Amazon has for years knowingly tricked people into signing up for Prime subscriptions. 'We have been deliberately confusing,' former employee says. Business Insider. https://www.businessinsider.com/amazon-prime-ftc-probe-customer-complaints-sign-ups-internal-documents-2022-3

18. Federal Trade Commission. (2023, March 23). FTC proposes rule provision making it easier for consumers to 'click to cancel' recurring subscriptions and memberships. Retrieved 25 May 2023 from https://www.ftc.gov/news-events/news/press-releases/2023/03/federal-trade-commission-proposes-rule-provision-making-it-easier-consumers-click-cancel-recurring

19. Biden, P. (2023, March 23). Too often, companies make it difficult to unsubscribe from a service [Tweet]. Twitter. Retrieved 25 May 2023 from https://twitter.com/POTUS/status/1638896377353601028

20. FORCED ACTION

1. Brignull, H. (2010, October). Privacy zuckering: A type of deceptive design. Retrieved 11 October 2022 from https://www.deceptive.design/types/privacy-zuckering
2. Krebs, B. (2022, August 13). Twitter. Retrieved 11 October 2022 from https://twitter.com/briankrebs/status/1558441625197633537
3. Screenshot used in figure captured from the Skype iPad app on 11 October 2022.
4. Screenshot used in figure captured from the Skype iPad app on 11 October 2022.
5. Hartzog, W. (2018, April 9). Privacy's blueprint: The battle to control the design of new technologies (illustrated). Harvard University Press.
6. Wylie, C. (2020). Mindf*ck: Cambridge Analytica and the plot to break America. Penguin Random House.
7. Griffith, C. (2019, February 18). Skype's sneaky contact harvest. The Australian. Retrieved 11 October 2022 from https://amp.theaustralian.com.au/business/technology/skypes-sneaky-contact-harvest/news-story/96fce90cc-fa81fe8929e218bc24414cf
8. Add similar segments to your targeting - Google Ads Help. (n.d.). Retrieved June 29, 2023, from https://support.google.com/google-ads/answer/7139569?hl=en-GB
9. Meta. (n.d.). About lookalike audiences. Facebook. Retrieved 28 May 2023 from https://www.facebook.com/business/help/164749007013531?id=401668390442328
10. Perkins v. Linkedin Corp. (Case No. 13-CV-04303-LHK). (2013, September 17). archive.org. Retrieved June 30, 2023, from http://ia800900.us.archive.org/6/items/gov.uscourts.cand.270092/gov.uscourts.cand.270092.96.1.pdf
11. Schlosser, D. (2015, June 5). LinkedIn dark patterns, or: why your friends keep spamming you to sign up for LinkedIn. Medium. Retrieved 4 April 2023 from https://medium.com/@danrschlosser/linkedin-dark-patterns-3ae726fe1462
12. Brignull, H. (2010). Friend spam: A type of deceptive design. Retrieved 1 January 2023 from https://old.deceptive.design/friend_spam/

21. HOW DECEPTIVE PATTERNS CAN BE MORE HARMFUL WHEN COMBINED

1. Luguri, J., & Strahilevitz, L.J. (2021, January 1). Shining a light on dark patterns. Journal of Legal Analysis, 13(1), 43–109. https://academic.oup.com/jla/article/13/1/43/6180579
2. The acceptance rates were as follows (treating drop-outs as rejecting data protection plan). Control group: 11.3% (73 people); Mild dark pattern group: 25.4% (155 people); Aggressive dark pattern group: 37.2% (217 people)
3. Strahilevitz, L. (2022, August 12). Update on Dark Patterns at the NIAC 2022 Summer National Meeting. niac.org. Retrieved October 18, 2022, from https://content.naic.org/sites/default/files/national_meeting/Lior+Update+on+Dark+Patterns.pdf

IV. HARMS CAUSED BY DECEPTIVE PATTERNS

1. European Commission, Directorate-General for Justice and Consumers, Lupiáñez-Villanueva, F., Boluda, A., Bogliacino, F. (2022). *Behavioural study on unfair commercial practices in the digital environment : dark patterns and manipulative personalisation : final report*, Publications Office of the European Union. **https://data.europa.eu/doi/10.2838/859030**

2. Servicio Nacional del Consumidor [SERNAC]. (2022, March). Policy Paper On Cookies Consent Requests:Experimental Evidence Of Privacy By Default And Dark Patterns On Consumer Privacy Decision Making. Retrieved January 28, 2023, from https://icpen.org/sites/default/files/2022-05/SERNAC_Policy_Paper_Cookies_-Experiment.pdf

3. Moser, C., S. Schoenebeck and P. Resnick (2019), 'Impulse buying: Design practices and consumer
    needs', Proceedings of the 2019 CHI Conference on Human Factors in Computing Systems (CHI '19),
        https://doi.org/10.1145/3290605.3300472

4. Soe, T. H., Nordberg, O. E., Guribye, F., & Slavkovik, M. (2020). Circumvention by design - dark patterns in cookie consent for online news outlets. Proceedings of the 11th Nordic Conference on Human-Computer Interaction: Shaping Experiences, Shaping Society. https://doi.org/10.1145/3419249.3420132

5. Consumer protection: manipulative online practices found on 148 out of 399 online shops screened. (2023, January 30). European Commission. https://ec.europa.eu/commission/presscorner/detail/en/ip_23_418

6. Dark commercial patterns. (2022). OECD Digital Economy Papers. https://doi.org/10.1787/44f5e846-en

7. In this research paper, Mathur et al refer to the perspectives as 'Lenses': Mathur, A., Kshirsagar, M., & Mayer, J. (2021). What Makes a Dark Pattern. . . Dark? Proceedings of the 2021 CHI Conference on Human Factors in Computing Systems. https://doi.org/10.1145/3411764.3445610

22. HARM TO INDIVIDUALS

1. Locked In: Consumer issues with subscription traps. (2016, March 8). Citizen's Advice. https://www.citizensadvice.org.uk/about-us/our-work/policy/policy-research-topics/consumer-policy-research/consumer-policy-research/locked-in-consumer-issues-with-subscription-traps/

2. Brignull, H., Leiser, M., Santos, C., & Doshi, K. (2023, April 25). Deceptive patterns – Legal cases. Retrieved April 25, 2023, from https://www.deceptive.design/cases

3. Lupiáñez-Villanueva, F., Boluda, A., Bogliacino, F., Liva, G., Lechardoy, L., & Rodríguez de las Heras Ballell, T. (2022). Behavioural study on unfair commercial practices in the digital environment: Dark patterns and manipulative personalisation. European Commission. https://op.europa.eu/en/publication-detail/-/publication/606365bc-d58b-11ec-a95f-01aa75ed71a1/language-en/format-PDF/source-257599418

4. Leiser, M. R., & Caruana, M. (2021). Dark Patterns: Light to be found in Europe's Consumer Protection Regime. Journal Of European Consumer And Market Law, 10(6),

237-251. Retrieved from https://hdl.handle.net/1887/3278362

5. Servicio Nacional del Consumidor [SERNAC]. (2022, March). Policy Paper On Cookies Consent Requests:Experimental Evidence Of Privacy By Default And Dark Patterns On Consumer Privacy Decision Making. Retrieved January 28, 2023, from https://icpen.org/sites/default/files/2022-05/SERNAC_Policy_Paper_Cookies_-Experiment.pdf

6. Shaw, S. (2019, June 12). Consumers Are Becoming Wise to Your Nudge - Behavioral Scientist. Behavioral Scientist. https://behavioralscientist.org/consumers-are-becoming-wise-to-your-nudge/

7. Lupiáñez-Villanueva, F., Boluda, A., Bogliacino, F., Liva, G., Lechardoy, L., & Rodríguez de las Heras Ballell, T. (2022). Behavioural study on unfair commercial practices in the digital environment: Dark patterns and manipulative personalisation. European Commission. https://op.europa.eu/en/publication-detail/-/publication/606365bc-d58b-11ec-a95f-01aa75ed71a1/language-en/format-PDF/source-257599418

8. Alegre, S. (2023). Freedom to Think: The Long Struggle to Liberate Our Minds. Atlantic Books (UK).

9. Alegre, S. (2022, April 25). Freedom to Think, by Susie Alegre - The Conduit. The Conduit. Retrieved May 28, 2023, from https://www.theconduit.com/insights/peace-justice/freedom-to-think-by-susie-alegre/

10. Article 9: Freedom of thought, belief and religion | Equality and Human Rights Commission. (1995). Retrieved May 28, 2023, from https://www.equalityhumanrights.com/en/human-rights-act/article-9-freedom-thought-belief-and-religion

23. HARM TO GROUPS IN SOCIETY

1. Luguri, J., & Strahilevitz, L. J. (2021, January 1). Shining a light on dark patterns. Journal of Legal Analysis, 13(1), 43–109. https://academic.oup.com/jla/article/13/1/43/6180579

2. Federal Trade Commission. (2022, September 15). Bringing dark patterns to light - FTC staff report. Retrieved 1 January 2023 from https://www.ftc.gov/reports/bringing-dark-patterns-light

3. Pak, K., & Shadel, D. (2011). AARP Foundation national fraud victim study. AARP Foundation. Retrieved 6 June 2023 from https://www.aarp.org/content/dam/aarp/research/surveys_statistics/econ/2011/2011-aarp-national-fraud-victim-study.pdf

25. OUR ATTEMPTS SO FAR HAVE NOT BEEN SUCCESSFUL

1. ACM Ethics. (2018, July 17). Case: Dark UX patterns. Association for Computing Machinery's committee on professional ethics. https://ethics.acm.org/code-of-ethics/using-the-code/case-dark-ux-patterns/

2. AIGA Standards of Professional Practice. (n.d.). AIGA. https://www.aiga.org/resources/aiga-standards-of-professional-practice

3. American Psychological Association. (2017). Ethical principles of psychologists and code of conduct. Retrieved 21 December 2022 from https://www.apa.org/ethics/code

4. UXPA code of professional conduct. (2019, April 14). UXPA International. https://uxpa.org/uxpa-code-of-professional-conduct/

5. European Union. (2005, May 11). Directive 2005/29/EC of the European Parliament and of the Council ('Unfair Commercial Practices Directive'). EUR-Lex. Retrieved 13 May 2023 from https://eur-lex.europa.eu/legal-content/EN/TXT/HTML/?uri=CELEX:32005L0029

6. European Union. (2021, December 29). Commission notice: Guidance on the interpretation and application of Directive 2005/29/EC of the European Parliament and of the Council concerning unfair business-to-consumer commercial practices in the internal market. EUR-Lex. Retrieved 13 May 2023 from https://eur-lex.europa.eu/legal-content/EN/TXT/?uri=CELEX:52021XC1229(05)

7. Truong, H., & Dalbard, A. (2022, June 30). Bright patterns as an ethical approach to counteract dark patterns. Retrieved 17 January 2023 from https://www.diva-portal.org/smash/get/diva2:1680425/FULLTEXT01.pdf

8. https://fairpatterns.com/ (coming soon from Amurabi: https://www.a-murabi.eu/).

9. ISO. (2019, July). ISO 9241-210:2019 Ergonomics of human-system interaction — Part 210: Human-centred design for interactive systems. ISO. Retrieved 17 January 2023 from https://www.iso.org/standard/77520.html

10. IAB Europe. (n.d.). Transparency and Consent Framework. Retrieved 21 March 2023 from https://iabeurope.eu/transparency-consent-framework/

11. GDPR.eu. (2018, November 16). Article 4 GDPR: Definitions. GDPR.eu. Retrieved 22 December 2022 from https://gdpr.eu/article-4-definitions/

12. Santos, C., Nouwens, M., Toth, M. J., Bielova, N., & Roca, V. (2021). Consent management platforms under the GDPR: Processors and/or controllers? Social Science Research Network. https://doi.org/10.2139/ssrn.4205933

13. Soe, T. H., Nordberg, O. E., Guribye, F., & Slavkovik, M. (2020, October). Circumvention by design: Dark patterns in cookie consent for online news outlets. Proceedings of the 11th Nordic conference on human–computer interaction: Shaping experiences, shaping society. https://doi.org/10.1145/3419249.3420132

14. Lomas, N. (2022, February 2). Behavioral ad industry gets hard reform deadline after IAB's TCF found to breach Europe's GDPR. Techcrunch. Retrieved 22 December 2022 from https://techcrunch.com/2022/02/02/iab-tcf-gdpr-breaches/

15. Santos, C., Nouwens, M., Toth, M. J., Bielova, N., & Roca, V. (2021). Consent management platforms under the GDPR: Processors and/or controllers? Social Science Research Network. https://doi.org/10.2139/ssrn.4205933

16. Walshe, P. (2023, March 29). All based on the IAB TCF. Having the IAB in charge of ad standards aka the TCF is like having Dracula in charge of the national blood bank. [Tweet] Twitter. Retrieved 29 March 2023 from https://twitter.com/Privacy-Matters/status/1641089844033249281

17. NOYB. (2023, January 24). Data protection authorities support NOYB's call for fair yes/no cookie banners. noyb.eu. Retrieved 27 May 2023 from https://noyb.eu/en/data-protection-authorities-support-noybs-call-fair-yesno-cookie-banners

27. LEGISLATION IN THE EUROPEAN UNION

1. European Union. (2005, May 11). Directive 2005/29/EC of the European Parliament and of the Council ('Unfair Commercial Practices Directive'). EUR-Lex. Retrieved 13

May 2023 from https://eur-lex.europa.eu/legal-content/EN/TXT/HTML/?uri=CELEX:32005L0029

2. All of the current EU laws described in this section are retained in the UK at the time of writing, though this is likely to change in the future.

3. Association for Computing Machinery (ACM). (2018). ACM Code of Ethics and Professional Conduct. Retrieved 31 March 2023 from https://www.acm.org/code-of-ethics

4. European Union. (2016, April 27). *Consolidated text: Regulation (EU) 2016/679 of the European Parliament and of the Council of 27 April 2016 on the protection of natural persons with regard to the processing of personal data and on the free movement of such data, and repealing Directive 95/46/EC (General Data Protection Regulation).* EUR-Lex. Retrieved March 27, 2024, from https://eur-lex.europa.eu/legal-content/EN/TXT/?uri=CELEX%3A02016R0679-20160504

5. European Union. (2022, May 28). *Consolidated text: Directive 2011/83/EU of the European Parliament and of the Council of 25 October 2011 on consumer rights, amending Council Directive 93/13/EEC and Directive 1999/44/EC of the European Parliament and of the Council and repealing Council Directive 85/577/EEC and Directive 97/7/EC of the European Parliament and of the Council ('Consumer Rights Directive').* EUR-Lex. Retrieved March 27, 2024, from https://eur-lex.europa.eu/legal-content/EN/TXT/?uri=CELEX%3A02011L0083-20220528

6. European Union. (2022, May 28). *Consolidated text: Council Directive 93/13/EEC of 5 April 1993 on unfair terms in consumer contracts.* EUR-Lex. Retrieved March 27, 2024, from https://eur-lex.europa.eu/eli/dir/1993/13/2022-05-28

7. European Union. (2018, November 14). *Directive (EU) 2018/1808 of the European Parliament and of the Council of 14 November 2018 amending Directive 2010/13/EU on the coordination of certain provisions laid down by law, regulation or administrative action in Member States concerning the provision of audiovisual media services (Audiovisual Media Services Directive) in view of changing market realities.* EUR-Lex. Retrieved March 27, 2024, from https://eur-lex.europa.eu/eli/dir/2018/1808/oj

8. European Union. (2000, June 8). *Directive 2000/31/EC of the European Parliament and of the Council of 8 June 2000 on certain legal aspects of information society services, in particular electronic commerce, in the Internal Market (Directive on electronic commerce).* EUR-Lex. Retrieved March 27, 2024, from https://eur-lex.europa.eu/eli/dir/2000/31/oj

9. European Union. (2009, December 19). *Consolidated text: Directive 2002/58/EC of the European Parliament and of the Council of 12 July 2002 concerning the processing of personal data and the protection of privacy in the electronic communications sector (Directive on privacy and electronic communications).* EUR-Lex. https://eur-lex.europa.eu/eli/dir/2002/58/2009-12-19

28. LEGISLATION IN THE UNITED STATES

1. Federal Trade Commission. (2022, September 15). Bringing dark patterns to light - FTC staff report. Retrieved 1 January 2023 from https://www.ftc.gov/reports/bringing-dark-patterns-light

2. CPDPConferences. (2022, June 3). Manipulative design practices online: Policy solutions for the EU and the US [Video]. YouTube. https://www.youtube.com/watch?v=kLU3w2tp3YA

29. ENFORCEMENT CHALLENGES

1. Vinocur, N. (2019, April 24). How one country blocks the world on data privacy. Politico. Retrieved 27 May 2023 from https://www.politico.com/story/2019/04/24/ireland-data-privacy-1270123
2. Bryant, J. (2023, January 4). Irish DPC fines Meta 390m euros over legal basis for personalized ads. International Association of Privacy Professionals. https://iapp.org/news/a/irish-dpc-fines-meta-390m-euros-over-legal-basis-for-personalized-ads/
3. Bracy, J. (2023, May 22). Meta fined GDPR-record 1.2 billion euros in data transfer case. International Association of Privacy Professionals. https://iapp.org/news/a/meta-fined-gdpr-record-1-2-billion-euros-in-data-transfer-case/
4. European Union. (2019, December 18). Directive (EU) 2019/2161 of the European Parliament and of the Council of 27 November 2019 amending Council Directive 93/13/EEC and Directives 98/6/EC, 2005/29/EC and 2011/83/EU of the European Parliament and of the Council as regards the better enforcement and modernisation of Union consumer protection rules (Text with EEA relevance). Retrieved 31 May 2023 from https://eur-lex.europa.eu/eli/dir/2019/2161/oj
5. Laubheimer, P. (2020, June 21). 3 persona types: Lightweight, qualitative, and statistical. Nielsen Norman Group. Retrieved 21 March 2023 from https://www.nngroup.com/articles/persona-types/
6. Lewis, C., Polson, P.G., Wharton, C., & Rieman, J. (1990, March). Testing a walkthrough methodology for theory-based design of walk-up-and-use interfaces. Proceedings of the conference on human factors in computing systems (pp. 235–242). Retrieved 5 July 2020 from https://doi.org/10.1145/97243.97279
7. Mozilla. (n.d.). Take screenshots on Firefox | Firefox Help. https://support.mozilla.org/en-US/kb/take-screenshots-firefox
8. NocoDB (n.d.). Retrieved 29 December 2022 from https://www.nocodb.com/
9. Baserow (n.d.). Retrieved 29 December 2022 from https://baserow.io/
10. Airtable (n.d.). Retrieved 29 December 2022 from https://www.airtable.com/
11. BrowserStack. (n.d.). Retrieved 8 January 2023 from https://www.browserstack.com/live
12. Brandwatch. (n.d.). Retrieved 27 May 2023 from https://www.brandwatch.com/
13. Mentionlytics. (n.d.). Retrieved 27 May 2023 from https://www.mentionlytics.com/
14. Bose, S. (2023, February 13). How to take screenshot in Selenium WebDriver. BrowserStack. https://www.browserstack.com/guide/take-screenshots-in-selenium
15. Carter, L. (n.d.). Air/shots: Discovering a workflow for app screenshots. Airbnb Design. https://airbnb.design/airshots-discovering-a-workflow-for-app-screenshots/
16. NOYB. (n.d.). WeComply. Retrieved 27 May 2023 from https://wecomply.noyb.eu/
17. NOYB. (2021, May 31). NOYB aims to end 'cookie banner terror' and issues more than 500 GDPR complaints. noyb.eu. Retrieved 27 May 2023 from https://noyb.eu/en/noyb-aims-end-cookie-banner-terror-and-issues-more-500-gdpr-complaints
18. BEUC. (2022, July 2). 'Dark patterns' and the EU consumer law acquis: Recommendations for better enforcement and reform. Retrieved 28 March 2023 from https://www.beuc.eu/sites/default/files/publications/beuc-x-2022-013_dark_patters_paper.pdf

VI. THE ROAD AHEAD

1. Leiser, M.R. (2020, June 12). 'Dark patterns': The case for regulatory pluralism. Social Science Research Network. https://doi.org/10.2139/ssrn.3625637
2. Directorate-General for Justice and Consumers (European Commission), Lupiáñez-Villanueva, F., Boluda, A., Bogliacino, F., Liva, G., Lechardoy, L., & Rodríguez de las Heras Ballell, T. (2022, May 16). Behavioural study on unfair commercial practices in the digital environment: Dark patterns and manipulative personalisation, final report. Publications Office of the European Union. https://data.europa.eu/doi/10.2838/859030
3. Mathur, A., Kshirsagar, M., & Mayer, J. (2021). What makes a dark pattern… dark? Proceedings of the 2021 CHI conference on human factors in computing systems. https://doi.org/10.1145/3411764.3445610
4. Himes, J.L., & Crevier, J. (2021, August). 'Something is happening here but you don't know what it is. Do you, Mrs. Jones?' Dark patterns as an antitrust violation. CPI Antitrust Chronicle. Retrieved 2 January 2023 from https://www.competitionpolicyinternational.com/wp-content/uploads/2021/08/7-Something-Is-Happening-Here-but-You-Dont-Know-What-It-Is.-Do-You-Mrs.-Jones-Dark-Patterns-as-an-Antitrust-Violation-By-Jay-L.-Himes-Jon-Crevier.pdf

30. CHANGES AFOOT IN THE EUROPEAN UNION

1. European Union. (2022, October 12). Regulation (EU) 2022/1925 of the European Parliament and of the Council of 14 September 2022 on contestable and fair markets in the digital sector and amending Directives (EU) 2019/1937 and (EU) 2020/1828 (Digital Markets Act). Retrieved 5 January 2023 from https://eur-lex.europa.eu/legal-content/EN/TXT/HTML/?uri=CELEX:32022R1925
2. The criteria have been simplified here for the sake of brevity. This Q&A from the European Commission provides more details: https://ec.europa.eu/commission/presscorner/detail/en/qanda_20_2349
3. European Commission. (2023, May 2). Questions and answers: Digital Markets Act: Ensuring fair and open digital markets. https://ec.europa.eu/commission/presscorner/detail/en/QANDA_20_2349
4. European Union. (2022, October 27). Regulation (EU) 2022/2065 of the European Parliament and of the Council of 19 October 2022 on a single market for digital services and amending Directive 2000/31/EC (Digital Services Act). Retrieved 5 January 2023 from https://eur-lex.europa.eu/legal-content/EN/TXT/HTML/?uri=CELEX:32022R2065
5. European Union. (2021, December 29). Commission notice: Guidance on the interpretation and application of Directive 2005/29/EC of the European Parliament and of the Council concerning unfair business-to-consumer commercial practices in the internal market. EUR-Lex. Retrieved 1 January 2023 from https://eur-lex.europa.eu/legal-content/EN/TXT/?uri=CELEX:52021XC1229(05)

31. CHANGES AFOOT IN THE UNITED STATES

1. Federal Trade Commission. (2021, June 15). Lina M Khan sworn in as chair of the FTC. Federal Trade Commission. https://www.ftc.gov/news-events/news/press-releases/2021/06/lina-m-khan-sworn-chair-ftc

2. Federal Trade Commission. (2022, December 19). Fortnite video game maker Epic Games to pay more than half a billion dollars over FTC allegations of privacy violations and unwanted charges. Federal Trade Commission. Retrieved 2 January 2023 from https://www.ftc.gov/news-events/news/press-releases/2022/12/fortnite-video-game-maker-epic-games-pay-more-half-billion-dollars-over-ftc-allegations

3. Federal Trade Commission. (2022, September 15). Bringing Dark Patterns to Light - FTC staff report. Retrieved 1 January 2023 from https://www.ftc.gov/reports/bringing-dark-patterns-light

4. Federal Trade Commission. (2022, November 3). FTC action against Vonage results in $100 million to customers trapped by illegal dark patterns and junk fees when trying to cancel service. Federal Trade Commission. Retrieved 31 May 2023 from https://www.ftc.gov/news-events/news/press-releases/2022/11/ftc-action-against-vonage-results-100-million-customers-trapped-illegal-dark-patterns-junk-fees-when-trying-cancel-service

5. Castro, D. (2023, January 4). The FTC's efforts to label practices 'dark patterns' is an attempt at regulatory overreach that will ultimately hurt consumers. ITIF. Retrieved 8 January 2023 from https://itif.org/publications/2023/01/04/the-ftcs-efforts-to-label-practices-dark-patterns-is-an-attempt-at-regulatory-overreach-that-will-hurt-consumers/

6. Federal Trade Commission. (2022, December 19). Fortnite video game maker Epic Games to pay more than half a billion dollars over FTC allegations of privacy violations and unwanted charges. Federal Trade Commission. Retrieved 2 January 2023 from https://www.ftc.gov/news-events/news/press-releases/2022/12/fortnite-video-game-maker-epic-games-pay-more-half-billion-dollars-over-ftc-allegations

32. AI, HYPERNUDGING AND SYSTEM-LEVEL DECEPTIVE PATTERNS

1. Pasternack, A. (2023, February 22). GPT-powered deepfakes are a 'powder keg.' Fast Company. https://www.fastcompany.com/90853542/deepfakes-getting-smarter-thanks-to-gpt

2. Hsu, T., & Thompson, S.A. (2023, February 8). Disinformation researchers raise alarms about A.I. chatbots. The New York Times. https://www.nytimes.com/2023/02/08/technology/ai-chatbots-disinformation.html

3. Knight, W. (2021, May 24). GPT-3 can write disinformation now—and dupe human readers. Wired. https://www.wired.com/story/ai-write-disinformation-dupe-human-readers/

4. Midjourney. (n.d.). Retrieved 30 May 2023 from https://www.midjourney.com/

5. DALL·E 2. (n.d.). https://openai.com/product/dall-e-2

6. Uizard Autodesigner (n.d.). Uizard. Retrieved 30 May 2023 from https://uizard.io/autodesigner/

7. AI-powered website and UI builder using OpenAi generated code. (n.d.). TeleportHQ. Retrieved 30 May 2023 from https://teleporthq.io/ai-website-builder

8. Uizard. (2023, April 12). Uizard Autodesigner full walkthrough [Video]. YouTube. https://www.youtube.com/watch?v=PD5j7Ll7wLs
9. Miles, K. (2014, August 22). Artificial intelligence may doom the human race within a century, Oxford professor says. HuffPost. https://www.huffpost.com/entry/artificial-intelligence-oxford_n_5689858
10. Meta Business Help Centre. (n.d.). About automated ads. Facebook. Retrieved 30 May 2023 from https://www.facebook.com/business/help/223852498347426?id=2393014447396453
11. Google Ads Help. (n.d.). About smart bidding and smart creative solutions with Google Ads. https://support.google.com/google-ads/answer/9297584?hl=en-GB
12. Kaptein, M. (2015). Persuasion profiling: How the internet knows what makes you tick. Business Contact.
13. Yeung, K. (2017). 'Hypernudge': Big Data as a mode of regulation by design. Information, Communication & Society, 20(1), 118–136. https://doi.org/10.1080/1369118x.2016.1186713
14. Kaptein, M. (2015). Persuasion profiling: How the internet knows what makes you tick. Business Contact.
15. Cialdini, R.B. (2006). Influence: The psychology of persuasion, revised edition. Harper Business.
16. Image source for figure: Kaptein, M., Markopoulos, P., de Ruyter, B., & Aarts, E. (2015). Personalizing persuasive technologies: Explicit and implicit personalization using persuasion profiles. International Journal of Human–Computer Studies, 77, 38–51. https://doi.org/10.1016/j.ijhcs.2015.01.004
17. Wylie, C. (2020). Mindf*ck: Cambridge Analytica and the plot to break America. Penguin Random House.
18. Leiser, M.R., & Santos, C. (2023, April 27). Dark patterns, enforcement, and the emerging digital design acquis: Manipulation beneath the interface. Social Science Research Network. https://papers.ssrn.com/sol3/papers.cfm?abstract_id=4431048

33. THE RISK OF A TECHNO-DYSTOPIAN FUTURE

1. Greenberg, S., Boring, S., Vermeulen, J., & Dostal, J. (2014, June 21). Dark patterns in proxemic interactions. Proceedings of the 2014 conference on designing interactive systems. https://doi.org/10.1145/2598510.2598541
2. Design Studio S. (n.d.). Retrieved 8 January 2023 from http://www.design-ss.com/product.html/JR/JR.html
3. Hon, A. (2022). You've been played: How corporations, governments, and schools use games to control us all. Basic Books.
4. Castro, D. (2023, January 4). The FTC's efforts to label practices 'dark patterns' is an attempt at regulatory overreach that will ultimately hurt consumers. ITIF. Retrieved 8 January 2023 from https://itif.org/publications/2023/01/04/the-ftcs-efforts-to-label-practices-dark-patterns-is-an-attempt-at-regulatory-overreach-that-will-hurt-consumers/

34. CONCLUDING THOUGHTS

1. Albrecht, L. (2018, February 20). Richard Thaler, Nobel Prize-winning economist, says Wells Fargo is 'slimy'. MarketWatch. https://www.marketwatch.com/story/richard-thaler-nobel-prize-winning-economist-says-wells-fargo-is-slimy-2018-02-16

EPILOGUE

1. Brignull, H., Leiser, M., Santos, C., & Doshi, K. (2023, April 25). Deceptive patterns: User interfaces designed to trick you. deceptive.design. Retrieved 25 April 2023 from https://www.deceptive.design/

Made in United States
Troutdale, OR
05/02/2024

19612541R00153